Elite · 125

Samurai Comma

940–1576

Stephen Turnbull · Illustrated by Richard Hook

Consultant editor Martin Windrow

First published in Great Britain in 2005 by Osprey Publishing
Midland House, West Way, Botley, Oxford OX2 0PH, United Kingdom
Email: info@ospreypublishing.com

© 2005 Osprey Publishing Ltd

All rights reserved. Apart from any fair dealing for the purpose of private study,
research, criticism or review, as permitted under the Copyright, Designs and
Patents Act, 1988, no part of this publication may be reproduced, stored in
a retrieval system, or transmitted in any form or by any means, electronic,
electrical, chemical, mechanical, optical, photocopying, recording or otherwise,
without the prior written permission of the copyright owner. Enquiries should
be addressed to the Publishers.

CIP data for this publication is available from the British Library.

ISBN 1 84176 743 3

Editor: Ruth Sheppard
Design: Alan Hamp
Index by David Worthington
Originated by The Electronic Page Company, Cwmbran, UK
Printed in China through World Print Ltd.

05 06 07 08 09 10 9 8 7 6 5 4 3 2 1

FOR A CATALOGUE OF ALL BOOKS PUBLISHED BY
OSPREY PLEASE CONTACT:

The Marketing Manager, Osprey Direct UK, PO Box 140
Wellingborough, Northants NN8 2FA, United Kingdom
Email: info@ospreydirect.co.uk

Osprey Direct USA, 2427 Bond Street,
University Park, IL 60466, USA
E-mail: info@ospreydirectusa.com

www.ospreypublishing.com

Dedication

To Chris and Christine Pike, with thanks for many years of friendship.

Acknowledgements

I wish to thank the many individuals and organizations in Japan and elsewhere who have helped in the preparation of this book, in particular my daughter Kate, who now handles the administrative side of my work in worthy succession to her mother.

Author's Note

This book discusses the military geniuses who achieved success in the fiendish task of commanding a samurai army, and I have tried to select the most outstanding examples of these personalities. In doing so I have attempted to avoid the traditional prejudices that automatically relegate certain samurai commanders to the second rank of achievement. Minamoto Yoshitsune appears in these pages, but so does Taira Tomomori, whom he defeated in his last battle. Kusunoki Masashige will be celebrated for his guerrilla skills in the mountains of Yoshino, but instead of telling of his defeat at Minatogawa, that episode will appear under the name of the victor, Ashikaga Takauji, whom rampant nationalism once condemned to the role of outcast and turncoat. His military skills are important here, not his politics.

Artist's Note

Readers may care to note that the original paintings from which the colour plates in this book were prepared are available for private sale. All reproduction copyright whatsoever is retained by the Publishers. All enquiries should be addressed to:

Scorpio Gallery, PO Box 475, Hailsham, East Sussex BN27 2SL

The Publishers regret that they can enter into no correspondence upon this matter.

Editor's Note

All photographs are from the author's collection unless otherwise stated.

SAMURAI COMMANDERS (1) 940–1561

INTRODUCTION

THE SAMURAI WERE the military aristocracy of old Japan. Fired by a code of individual honour and loyalty, they were an elite force among the fighting men of the medieval and early modern worlds. As the demands of honour placed upon them included the achievement of personal glory, this sometimes came into conflict with the overall need to win a battle, and a samurai might then pursue his own, sometimes selfish, ends. An army composed of samurai was therefore an extremely volatile entity. To organize such men effectively and to lead them into battle and on to victory consequently required very special qualities to be found only in certain outstanding characters. These were the samurai commanders. We come across them under various names and titles. Sometimes they are referred to as *taisho* (generals), often they are the *daimyo* (feudal lords), whom the individual samurai were pledged to serve until death. Whatever the name or guise, the samurai commanders were an elite among an elite, the *crème de la crème* of the samurai class.

Samurai warfare was never a static concept. New challenges, new technology and above all new opponents tested successive generations of samurai commanders over many centuries. For this reason the structure of this work will reflect the changing nature of the task of samurai leadership as it evolved over 500 years. The background to the biographies of the samurai commanders, which form the major part of this work, will therefore be the changing nature of samurai warfare itself.

Of all the changes that occurred in the conduct of samurai warfare, none was to have a longer-lasting impact than the infantry revolution of the mid-16th century. Often simplistically reduced to the introduction of firearms, this complex development of major changes in military thinking, planning and leadership led to a radically different model of samurai command. It was a process that took about three decades to filter

Minamoto Yoritomo (1147–99) led the Minamoto family in battle and was defeated in 1180 at the battle of Ishibashiyama, as shown in this print. After this he wisely left generalship to his talented brother Yoshitsune, whose victories won for Yoritomo the position of Shogun, the military dictator of Japan.

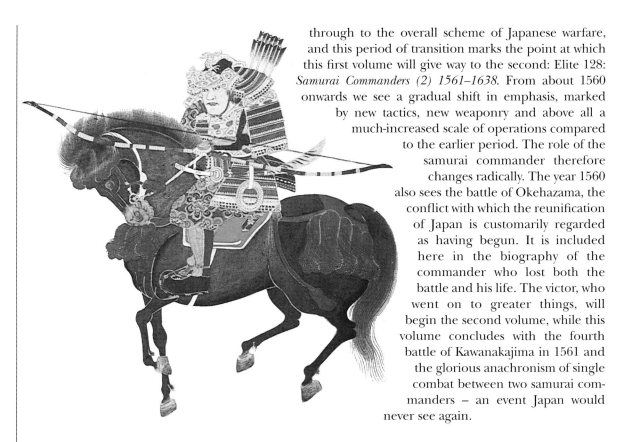

through to the overall scheme of Japanese warfare, and this period of transition marks the point at which this first volume will give way to the second: *Elite 128: Samurai Commanders (2) 1561–1638*. From about 1560 onwards we see a gradual shift in emphasis, marked by new tactics, new weaponry and above all a much-increased scale of operations compared to the earlier period. The role of the samurai commander therefore changes radically. The year 1560 also sees the battle of Okehazama, the conflict with which the reunification of Japan is customarily regarded as having begun. It is included here in the biography of the commander who lost both the battle and his life. The victor, who went on to greater things, will begin the second volume, while this volume concludes with the fourth battle of Kawanakajima in 1561 and the glorious anachronism of single combat between two samurai commanders – an event Japan would never see again.

The classic image of the mounted samurai general, identified in the original caption as a member of the Fujiwara family. The Fujiwara were the rivals of the Taira and the Minamoto at the time of the rise of the samurai.

THE FIRST SAMURAI AND THEIR COMMANDERS

The starting date for this study of samurai commanders is the year 940 because it was during that year at Kitayama in Shimosa province that the rebel leader Taira Masakado was killed in battle. Taira Masakado is the first individual commander of samurai to be known to us in any great detail. That he was well versed in the ways of the warrior comes over very clearly from a comment in *Konjaku Monogatari*, a *gunkimono* (collection of war tales). that includes a section dealing with his campaign. 'Masakado, along with his boon companions', writes the author, 'invariably dealt with any matter by having recourse to battle. He burned down many men's houses and he took many men's lives.' Just as in the *Shomonki*, another *gunkimono* that in this case deals exclusively with Masakado's rebellion, there is a recognition that great warriors possessed a particular form of commanding presence that both provided and displayed their leadership qualities. To the author of *Konjaku Monogatari*, admittedly, all samurai were 'mysterious, peculiar and hard to fathom'. They could not be judged by the standards of ordinary people. This was even truer in the case of samurai commanders. Such men were 'feared in the realm' and after some exploit 'all the more held in awe'.

The rebellion of Taira Masakado provides us with an early example of samurai warfare at a time when many of the traditions later to be associated with the samurai were only just beginning to be formulated.

The most important of these traditions, and the most relevant to the command of samurai, was the emphasis on the samurai as a mounted archer. The 'Way of the Warrior', enshrined many centuries later as the notion of *bushido*, was expressed in these times either as *kyuba no michi* (the way of the horse and the bow) or *kyusen no michi* (the way of the bow and arrow). Later literature and advances in technology would provide us with the idea of 'the sword as the soul of the samurai', but during the tenth century the bow was the samurai weapon *par excellence*. There is a curious confirmation of the relative attitudes towards swords and bows contained in one of the other stories of warriors that make up the *Konjaku Monogatari* collection. One night a certain Tachibana Norimitsu was attacked by some robbers when he was armed only with a sword: 'Norimitsu crouched down and looked around, but as he could not see any sign of a bow but only a great glittering sword, he thought with relief, "It's not a bow, at any rate".'

A samurai on foot, typical of the hundreds who served commanders such as Taira Masakado (*c.*903–40). Note the importance of the bow, and the spare bowstring carried on a wooden reel at the belt.

The primacy of the mounted archer role over that of swordsman was reflected in the costume and equipment worn by the samurai of Masakado's time. Although clumsy when fighting on foot, the box-like *yoroi* style of armour made the mounted warrior into a well-protected, if somewhat inflexible, 'gun platform'. In marked contrast to the chain mail that constituted the styles of armour worn on the other side of the world during the tenth century, the samurai's armour reflected its Asiatic origin in being composed of small scales laced together to make a strong but flexible composite plate. The armour scales were either of iron or of leather, combined in a pattern that concentrated the iron scales in areas where the most vital protection was needed. Horizontal rows of these scales were firmly laced together then lacquered as a protection against the weather. A set of these rows was then assembled to make the particular armour plate, the overall shape depending on which area of the body the section was to be worn. Thus the *sode* (shoulder plates) were large, almost square, constructions, while the *kusazuri* (skirt pieces) of the *do* (body armour) were trapezoidal in shape. The horizontal sections of the armour plates were joined together by means of vertical rows of thick silk cords, the colour and design of which gave the *yoroi* its instantly recognizable and attractive appearance.

The samurai commanders, naturally enough, wore the finest and most elaborate armours of all. These were sometimes referred to as *o-yoroi* (literally 'great armour'), ornamented with gilded fittings and rich leather. Although the *sode* have the appearance of shields, there does not appear to have been any heraldic significance in the Western sense of the often-elaborate patterns of colour for the lacing. Nor does there seem to be much justification for the claim that the colour red was reserved for generals. For example, in the *Heike Monogatari* account of the battle of Uji in 1180, we read of Ashikaga Matataro setting an example to his commander Taira Tomomori by leading the way into battle. Matataro's appearance is described as follows: 'Matataro, wearing armour with red leather lacing over a *hitatare* of russet gold brocade, with a helmet ornamented by lofty horns, a gold mounted *tachi* by his side, and twenty-four black and white spotted arrows on his back, carrying a black lacquered bow lashed with red bands...'

The samurai commanders who had the responsibility of controlling and using such enthusiasts as Ashikaga Matataro relied on a number of devices to ameliorate the daunting task. The most important device of all, that of social cohesion based on certain leadership ties, is illustrated very clearly in the Masakado saga two centuries earlier. Masakado's rebellion represents the coming-of-age of a provincial military elite capable of organizing itself under the leadership of an influential local samurai commander. In the extensive alliances formed by Masakado and his opponents we see the prototype of what were to become known as *bushidan* (warrior bands). These groups, which on the battlefield made up the samurai armies, cut across the established power structure that was centred on the imperial court in Kyoto. Kyoto was then called Heian, and gives its name to the Heian period in Japanese history (AD 794–1184), the age of the classical samurai warrior. The ties thus created for the samurai commanders were both social and military, and were encouraged by the expansion of the provincial aristocracy's developing role as the police and military delegates of a distant emperor.

These functions date from roughly the ninth century, when imperial commissions, initially to provide guards for the imperial palace in Kyoto, required strong local landowners to become 'those who serve', a fairly literal translation of the word 'samurai'. Taira Masakado was an outstanding, but by no means isolated, example of someone who tried to use that commission for his own ends, because it was not long before the new samurai commanders realized what power they possessed and what potential that gave them.

Samurai commanders with attendants. The contrast in appearance between the mounted warriors and their servants is very noticeable.

Masakado's prototype *bushidan* centred on the Toyota and Sashima districts of Shimosa province. Some of its members were his relatives; others were neighbours attracted to Masakado by his martial prowess and the prospect of self-enrichment. They were bound to Masakado by ties of mutual dependence and security, but at this stage in the development of a samurai command and social structure there were no formal contractual arrangements such as would develop over the following centuries. Nor were his successful followers automatically rewarded by their commander with fiefs or land rights. Also, unlike the later *bushidan*, the samurai who made up the core of Masakado's strength were few in number, perhaps less than 100, but he commanded such prestige that this 100 could easily become thousands.

The nature of the warfare into which the newly emerged samurai commanders led their followers was by no means invariably the formal, ordered and gentlemanly combat that the *gunkimono* sometimes imply. That such events actually happened may not easily be denied, and can be summed up as a sequence of honourable challenges contracted between worthy individuals. Theoretically, a battle should begin by the loosing of whistling signal arrows as an announcement to the *kami* (deities) that deeds of martial valour were about to commence. The individual samurai, who would compete for the honour of being the first into battle, should then seek out a worthy opponent. This was done by proclaiming one's pedigree and personal achievements in a loud voice from the saddle. An opponent of suitable status having been found, the two would commence an archery duel from horseback in an action that was a cross between two gunslingers in a Western movie and the traditional sport of *yabusame*, where warriors in hunting dress tried to hit targets at the gallop. The bow would then be exchanged for the *tachi* (sword), the sword for the *tanto* (dagger) until even bare hands might settle the outcome. In a bizarre ritual almost unique to Japan, the victor would then sever the head of the victim, and present it to his commander as the finest evidence of duty done.

The confusion of a battle situation did not provide many opportunities for such activities to proceed unhindered, so we may regard the majority of these accounts in the *gunkimono* as later romantic elaboration. More realistically, the samurai commander's main task consisted not in overseeing a number of simultaneous duels to the death, but in co-ordinating an attack plan that would ensure victory while still allowing his headstrong followers some opportunity to behave in this cherished manner. Analysis of the battle descriptions in the *gunkimono* paints a very different picture of the prevalent means of gaining victory. Karl Friday, in a paper cited in the bibliography, has worked out that out of 58 episodes recounted in various chronicles and *gunkimono* in sufficient detail to enable a conclusion to be drawn about their conduct, no fewer than 41 involved ambushes or surprise attacks. For example, *Hogen Monogatari*, the *gunkimono* concerned with the Hogen Rebellion of 1156, puts the following words into the mouth of the samurai commander Minamoto Tametomo: '...whether to break down strong positions though surrounded by enemies, or to destroy the enemy when attacking a fortified place, in any case there is nothing equal to a night attack to achieve victory. Therefore we bear down on the Takamatsu Palace immediately, set fire to it on three sides and hold them in check on the fourth side, those who escape the fire cannot escape arrows, and those who fear arrows cannot escape fire.' In a separate account translated by Friday, we read quite simply of a certain 'greatest warrior in the land', who 'was highly skilled in the conduct of battles, night attacks, archery duels on horseback and ambushes'. In other words the supposedly dishonourable activities are spoken of in the same breath as the supposedly noble ones.

Minamoto Tametomo (1139–70) took part in the Hogen Incident of 1156, a rebellion involving a rival candidate to the imperial throne. He was banished as a result and was exiled to the island of Oshima, where he is shown in this print. Tametomo was of Herculean strength and very skilled as an archer.

One final point needs to be made at this stage regarding the samurai commander's responsibilities on the battlefield. Although the *gunkimono* hardly credit the fact, he was also the leader of large numbers of foot soldiers clad in simple armour and wielding polearms such as the *naginata*, a glaive that resembled a wide, sword-bladed halberd on a long shaft. The correct command and use of foot soldiers, whose rough bewhiskered features frequently appear in the corners of scroll paintings of the period, was crucial to any victory being gained. They were the men who would actually set fire to buildings, who would maintain a wooden shield wall on a battlefield, and who would supposedly hold themselves back while their betters went about the honourable business of seeking an opponent considerably worthier than they.

One little-known weapon that was operated by these lower-class warriors was the *oyumi* or Japanese crossbow. It was chiefly employed during sieges of the wooden stockades that constituted early Japanese fortresses, and could fire either arrows or stones. A siege situation was all-out war, as we read in *Mutsu Waki* concerning the so-called 'Early Nine Years' War': 'The commander ordered his troops to enter the nearby village, demolish the houses and heap the wood in the moat around the stockade. He further told them to cut thatch and reeds and pile these along the riverbanks... The commander then took up a torch himself and threw it on the pyre...' The resulting conflagration was made much worse by the shafts and feathers of the hundreds of arrows loosed by the besiegers, which blanketed the outer towers and walls like the straws of a traditional raincoat. Just as in the *Hogen Monogatari* account above, the commander opened one side of the cordon to let the defenders escape from the fire, then ordered them to be shot down as they fled.

In spite of all the value attached to individual heroics, the skills of the successful samurai commander included tasks like setting fire to buildings and slaughtering their inhabitants as they emerged. Just such a scene is shown here.

Taira Masakado (c.903–40)

Having set the scene, let us examine the career of the first of our samurai commanders, who is believed to have been born in the year 903, although this date cannot be verified. As his surname implies, Masakado was of the Taira family, a clan descended from imperial stock that was one of the two major power blocs to develop over the tenth and eleventh centuries. In his youth Masakado served the imperial regent Fujiwara Tadahira in Kyoto, but returned in 931 to the Kanto, the fertile plain in eastern Japan where Tokyo now stands, and engaged in open warfare with local rivals. Some had the surname Taira, others Minamoto, the other great family that was currently rising to power. Masakado won a victory at the battle of Kawawa in 935, but was soundly defeated twice the following year, of which the author of the *Shomonki* attributes the first to the wrath of the gods and the second to an episode of *beriberi*, which rendered Masakado incapable of effective leadership.

The origins of Masakado's rebellion are complex, but the conflict appears to have begun when Masakado took the side of an unscrupulous district official called Okiyo Okimi in a dispute. His involvement escalated into a full-scale attack on government buildings. This seems to have given Masakado delusions of grandeur, leading him to annex Hitachi province and plan, with his ally, further conquests in the Kanto. At this point other samurai leaders were despatched by the government to defeat him. Two in particular took up the challenge. They were Taira Sadamori, an old enemy of Masakado's, and Fujiwara Hidesato. Masakado struck first, and in an unsavoury incident captured Sadamori's wife, who was raped by Masakado's soldiers before Masakado could intervene to save her. This made the enmity that much greater, and when Masakado and Hidesato met in battle the fighting was fierce. He was first defeated at Kawaguchi in 940, and two weeks later the final battle of his career took place.

The battle was fought at Kitayama (otherwise known as Kojima) in Shimosa province. Taira Masakado tried to ambush Taira Sadamori as he marched on Shimosa, but Sadamori entered the territory in force, burning the houses of Masakado's supporters, and destroying the mansion Masakado had built for himself. When the two forces met in battle the primacy of the samurai as a mounted archer comes over very clearly. There are also several clues as to the role adopted by a samurai commander in such a battle.

Both sides had erected lines of wooden shields as a defence against mounted attack. These shields were of simple board construction and had a hinged strut at the rear. But a high wind was blowing from the direction of Masakado's lines. It blew over the shield wall erected by his foot soldiers, and blew the corresponding shield line of his opponents into their faces. There followed a mounted action by the Fujiwara/Taira allies, to which Masakado responded by ordering a cavalry advance, but then the wind changed. The text of the *Shomonki* implies that this put Masakado's archers at a disadvantage. It is interesting to note that up to this point Masakado had been at the rear, but he then joined in the fray,

Minamoto Yoshiie (1041–1108), who learned the trade of the samurai commander alongside his father Yoriyoshi. He is wearing full samurai armour except for an *eboshi* (cap) instead of a helmet.

'he put on his helmet and armour, galloped his charger off to the front, and joined in the fighting himself. But the punishment of heaven was clearly visited upon him when his horse failed to fly like the wind…struck by a stray arrow from one of the gods, Masakado perished all alone…'

So died the first of our samurai commanders. Taira Masakado presents a personification of samurai warfare in its early stages, in which battles were simple affairs but where raiding and fire were equally as important in deciding the outcome of a campaign. We see less emphasis on individual skills. That was to come with the glory days of the Gempei Wars, when the exploits of ancestors such as Taira Masakado were to be invoked as suitable and stirring precedents.

Minamoto Yoriyoshi (995–1082)

Three family names in particular have been mentioned so far. These are Fujiwara, Taira and Minamoto. The first supplied many notable warriors during the Heian period, but the Fujiwara are better known as administrators. The other two names of Taira and Minamoto will dominate the discussion of samurai commanders over the next two centuries.

The first samurai to take the surname of Minamoto was Tsunemoto (894–961), who fought against Taira Masakado. He adopted the name in the year of his death, and it was with his great-grandson Yoriyoshi that the family began to achieve wide recognition. Yoriyoshi was born in 995 and fought under his father Yorinobu (968–1048). He came to individual prominence in the 'Early Nine Years' War', which was the result of Yoriyoshi's commission to suppress Abe Yoritoki, a man who had exploited his official position for personal gain. Yoritoki was killed in 1057, but his son Abe Sadato continued the fight from a wooden stockade in Kawasaki. The Minamoto attack failed, and when the Minamoto pulled back to regroup a fierce blizzard began. Abe Sadato launched an attack on them as they withdrew, and out of a fighting rearguard action few of the Minamoto survived. For his bravery during the retreat Yoriyoshi's 13-year-old son Yoshiie earned the honourable nickname of Hachimantaro – the first-born son of the war *kami* Hachiman. The *gunkimono Mutsu Waki*, a major source for the campaign, contains some fascinating insights into the qualities of leadership that Yoriyoshi possessed. Many men joined Yoriyoshi, we are told, 'because Yoriyoshi cared for them and saw to their needs'. After one particular battle, Yoriyoshi: 'fed his soldiers, and put their equipment in order. He personally went round the camp, tending to the wounded. The soldiers were deeply moved, and all said, "We will repay our obligations with our bodies"…'

In this woodblock print, Minamoto Yoshiie is identified by his nickname Hachimantaro, 'first born of Hachiman', bestowed upon him in recognition of his brave service.

In 1062 the Minamoto returned to the fray and besieged Abe Sadato in his fortress of Kuriyagawa. Again the fighting was fierce, and young Yoshiie is said to have uttered a prayer to his protective deity Hachiman that he would establish a shrine to him if victory were gained. Thus it was that on returning to Kyoto with the severed heads of his enemies, the Minamoto established the Tsurugaoka Hachiman shrine in Kamakura, the place that was to become the holiest of shrines for the Minamoto family. Minamoto Yoriyoshi died peacefully in 1082, satisfied that the glorious name was to be continued by Yoshiie.

Minamoto Yoshiie (1041–1108)

In 1083 Minamoto Yoriyoshi's son Yoshiie set off on campaign in an affair known as the 'Later Three Years' War'. Just like his father, Yoshiie was to become an excellent samurai commander, and certain incidents on the way showed Yoshiie's leadership skills very clearly. Once he observed a flock of geese arising in disorder from a forest, and concluded correctly that his enemy had laid an ambush. This was something he had

Yoshiie was always as popular with his men as his father had been, and here we see him eating with his men.

learned from a study of the Chinese military classics, evidence indeed of a professional approach to the command of samurai.

Much of the fighting during the Later Three Years' War consisted of a siege of the stockade fortress of Kanazawa. There was much opportunity for individual samurai glory during the repeated assaults, and at the close of each day's fighting Yoshiie examined his men's exploits. The bravest warrior was assigned to the 'bravery seat' while the worst at fighting had to occupy a 'cowardice seat'. Nevertheless, Yoshiie was always as popular with his men as his father had been, and the chronicle *Oshu Gosannen Ki* concentrates as much on Yoshiie's talents in command as his legendary fighting prowess. We read, for example, of him warming soldiers with his own body during the freezing winter campaigns, and even reviving some who appeared to have frozen to death.

But Minamoto Yoshiie also had to contend with very different problems off the battlefield. Unlike his father's official commission to go to war, the government never recognized Yoshiie's campaign as anything other than a private quarrel. So when the fortress of Kanazawa finally fell to a desperate attack there was no official recognition or reward for Yoshiie's bravery, and he is said to have thrown the severed heads of his enemies into a ditch. His political reputation never quite recovered from this act of disobedience. Minamoto Yoshiie spent the last years of his life living in Kyoto trying to regain a position in court. At that time warriors were still regarded as inferior beings compared to courtiers, and Yoshiie's peaceful death came as something of an anticlimax to his exciting campaign life. He was, however, regarded as the greatest warrior in the land, and at the time of his death a courtier wrote, 'His military authority filled the realm. Here was a man truly worthy of being a great general.'

SAMURAI COMMANDERS OF THE GEMPEI WARS

From wars, official or otherwise, against rebels challenging the imperial authority in the 11th century, we move to the commanders who fought for very different reasons during the 12th century. The two names of Minamoto and Taira will dominate this narrative as the rival clans tried to control the imperial government by marriage, political intrigue and ultimately force of arms. Two small-scale conflicts, the Hogen Rebellion of 1156 and the Heiji Rebellion of 1160, paved the way for the major set of actions known as the Gempei Wars, fought between 1180 and 1189.

Here we will encounter some of the greatest samurai commanders in all of Japanese history, who achieved names for themselves not only for their prowess on the battlefield, but for the traditions and exploits that their followers bequeathed to future generations.

The early years of the Taira/Minamoto rivalry are marked by the activities of two men who were to make an enormous political impact on the Japanese scene, but whose military exploits as samurai commanders were more limited. They were Taira Kiyomori and Minamoto Yoritomo. Kiyomori (1118–81) began his career as a renowned warrior, and was much admired by his followers for taking a stand against the warrior monks who periodically descended upon the capital, but it is as a statesman that he is best known. Minamoto Yoritomo (1147–99) led the Minamoto family in battle and was defeated in 1180 at the battle of Ishibashiyama. After this he wisely left generalship to his talented brother Yoshitsune, whose victories won for Yoritomo the position of Shogun, the military dictator of Japan. This was originally a title given to temporary imperial commissions. Yoritomo made it into a permanent post that existed until the mid-19th century.

Minamoto Yorimasa (1106–80)

The opening conflict of the Gempei Wars was launched by a veteran member of the Minamoto family called Minamoto Yorimasa. Yorimasa was renowned both as a samurai and as a poet, and was much in favour in the imperial court, having supposedly killed with an arrow a monster that was terrorizing the palace. Like Taira Kiyomori, Yorimasa had also stood up to the warrior monks, but earned their admiration when he showed great respect to the *mikoshi*, the sacred palanquin in which the *kami* was believed to dwell: 'Then Yorimasa quickly leapt from his horse, and taking off his helmet and rinsing his mouth with water, made humble obeisance before the sacred emblem, all his three hundred retainers likewise following his example.'

The monks hesitated in their attack, noting the presence of the respected (and respectful) Yorimasa, and his comparatively small army, and decided to attack another gate instead. Here no diplomatic general was waiting for them, but a hail of arrows from mounted samurai.

In 1180 Yorimasa took the part of the imperial claimant Prince Mochihito, who was the rival nominee for the throne against Antoku, the grandson of Taira Kiyomori. His main allies were the warrior monks of Nara and from Miidera temple near Kyoto. Yorimasa's plot was discovered by Kiyomori, who sent his son Taira Tomomori to apprehend him. Yorimasa, accompanied by the Miidera monks, hastily fled from Kyoto to join up with the Nara monks to the south. The main obstacle between Kyoto and Nara was the Uji River, so, as he was being pursued by the Taira, Yorimasa decided to rest for the night just south of the river. His men tore up the planking of the bridge and prepared for the dawn when they could continue their march to Nara.

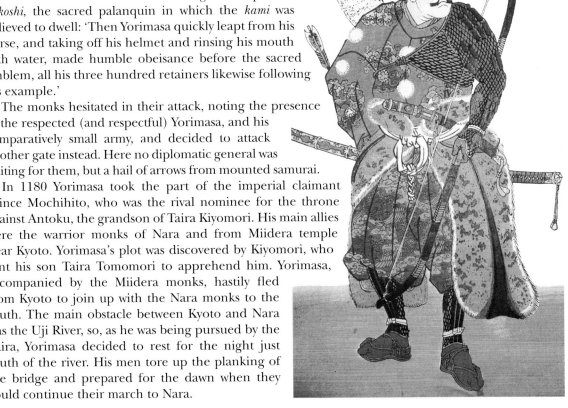

Taira Kiyomori (1118–81) began his career as a renowned warrior, we see him here dressed in hunting gear as an archer.

Up to this point Yorimasa had acted excellently as a commander of samurai. To place the wide Uji River between him and his pursuers was a sensible tactical move, and Yorimasa cannot be blamed for the determination of Taira Tomomori to crush his rebellion at all costs. So it was that as the dawn was breaking Taira samurai rode on to the broken bridge. Not suspecting that the planking had been removed, many fell to their deaths, while others began to fight their way across the framework. Here was fought a desperate rear-guard action by warrior monks from Miidera in a series of individual combats that have entered samurai legend. Though at first largely successful, they were finally thwarted when Tomomori ordered his samurai to swim the river on their horses. Driven back by overwhelming numbers, Yorimasa and his men sought temporary safety in the temple of Byodo-In, and when all was lost Yorimasa set an example to his men by performing the classic act of *hara-kiri*. He first wrote a poem on his war fan, and then cut his belly open. His sons took his head to prevent it from falling into the hands of their enemies.

As a samurai commander Yorimasa may not have been in the first league. To allow his rebellion to be overcome almost before it had started shows a lack of strategic planning and too great a reliance on his volatile monk allies. He is remembered best for his fighting retreat and classic suicide, an act that alone has placed him into the category of inspirational figures for generations of samurai that were to come.

TOP **A portrait of Minamoto Yoritomo, the first Minamoto Shogun and one of the most successful samurai leaders of all time.**
BELOW **Minamoto Yorimasa (1106–80) was renowned both as a samurai and as a poet, and was much in favour in the imperial court, having supposedly killed with an arrow a monster that was terrorizing the palace. This is the scene shown here.**

Minamoto Yoshinaka (1154–84)

So perished the veteran warrior of the Minamoto clan. It was now up to a younger generation to continue the struggle against the Taira, and it is Yoritomo's cousin Yoshinaka who first demands our attention. He was brought up in the Kiso Mountains of central Japan, so it is by the name of Kiso Yoshinaka that he is often known. Like Yorimasa he had responded to Prince Mochihito's ill-fated call to arms in 1180, but drew back from active campaigning as soon as the fate of Yorimasa reached his ears. In 1183 he reasserted his authority and went to war against the Taira. Yoshinaka's campaign was launched not from within the capital but directly north in the mountains bordering the Noto peninsula. The Taira responded, and marched north to confront Minamoto Yoshinaka. They first came upon a Minamoto outpost at Hiuchi, a simple stockade fortress that was built on rocky crags and well defended. The Minamoto had built a dam to create a moat, which hindered the Taira assault until a traitor fired an arrow with a note telling them how to breach the dam and run off the water. After this the fortress soon fell to the Taira.

源平宇治橋大合戰之圖

源三位入道頼政

源仲綱

Yorimasa at the first battle of Uji in 1180. Driven back by overwhelming numbers, he and his men sought temporary safety in the temple of Byodo-In, and when all was lost Yorimasa set an example to his men by performing the act of *hara-kiri*. He first wrote a poem on his war fan, and then cut his belly open.

In spite of this setback Yoshinaka's greatest victory was just around the corner, and Kurikara (otherwise known as Tonamiyama) became the battle by which the tide of the Gempei Wars turned in favour of the Minamoto. The Taira army that was pursuing Yoshinaka divided into two. The larger part, under Taira Koremori, crossed the pass of Kurikara and fought the battle. The smaller contingent entered Etchu province through Noto province further to the north, and gained a minor victory that was totally nullified by the defeat at Kurikara. Yoshinaka's army advanced to the pass of Kurikara from the east, and observed that the Taira were approaching the summit of Tonamiyama up the pass from the west. He erected 30 white banners about a mile away on Kurosaka hill to make the Taira think they would be faced with a vastly superior force when they descended. The trick worked, and the Taira decided to rest on the safety of the mountain and water their horses.

Yoshinaka divided his forces. One detachment was sent on a wide sweep to approach the Taira from the rear. Three units were selected to conceal themselves at the foot of Kurikara valley, which lay beneath the pass. The rest he held centrally. This force engaged the Taira in a long archery duel to cover their comrades' movements, providing one of the few occasions in samurai history when the classic samurai battle actually happened! This gave time for the other Minamoto contingents to prepare, and as the sun set Yoshinaka's encircling force arrived at the rear, well supplied with many more banners than would normally be carried by a small mobile force to give the impression of larger numbers. As the Taira reacted to this surprise they met a further shock in front. Yoshinaka's men had rounded up a herd of oxen and tied torches to their horns. The torches were fired and the enraged oxen whipped off along the pass. Some Taira samurai were knocked clean off the path by the frantic herd. The Taira were driven down into the valley and heavily defeated in the confusion.

Minamoto Kiso Yoshinaka (1154–84) is depicted here in a statue erected on the site of his greatest victory: the battle of Kurikara (Tonamiyama) in 1183.

Minamoto Kiso Yoshinaka lacked the political skills to transform his considerable military victories, which included the capture of Kyoto, into a permanent gain. This woodblock print portrays him looking very fierce.

A few days later, Kiso Yoshinaka defeated Taira Munemori, Koremori's uncle and joint commander on the march north, who had retreated following the Kurikara defeat, at the battle of Shinowara. The battle began with an archery duel between ten champions from each side, after which the fight became general. Several celebrated single combats took place here, and among the dead was Yoshinaka's old retainer, Saito Sanemori, who had dyed his hair black to appear younger.

With the Taira crushed in two engagements, nothing could prevent Yoshinaka from entering Kyoto as victor, but this aroused the jealousy of his cousin Yoritomo, who sent his brother Yoshitsune to apprehend Yoshinaka. At the second battle of Uji in 1184, Minamoto Yoshinaka used the river as a defence, but in reverse from the situation in 1180. Yoshitsune's army crossed the river on their horses to attack him. Two of Yoshitsune's samurai, Kajiwara Kagesue and Sasaki Takatsuna, both wanted to be the first into action, and raced each other across the river in an incident that became famous. Yoshinaka was defeated and pursued to nearby Awazu where he made a last stand accompanied by his most loyal companions. Kiso Yoshinaka was finally struck dead by an arrow when his horse became mired in a paddy field, and then his retainer Imai Kanehira committed honourable suicide by diving off his horse with his sword in his mouth.

Yoshinaka's most faithful companion also deserves mention. Tomoe Gozen, described in some accounts as Yoshinaka's wife or mistress, in others simply as a 'beautiful girl', provides a rare example of a female samurai warrior. She had fought beside him since his campaigns began, and did so at Uji, taking an enemy head in the battle. She would have fought to the last, but Yoshinaka insisted that she leave the field.

Minamoto Yoshinaka's career as a samurai commander was brief but glorious, like a rocket exploding in the night sky. His victory at Kurikara was a tactical masterpiece involving deception and initiative, as well as more traditional samurai skills. He also clearly inspired his men, and was served by a handful of devoted followers. But Yoshinaka's genius was limited to the battlefield situation. The behaviour of his troops, and his own unwillingness to play the role of courtier, aroused strong resentment when he entered Kyoto and led to calls for his downfall. Yoshinaka thereby played straight into his wily cousin's hands. Had it not been for the political genius of Yoritomo, which contrasted markedly with Yoshinaka's political naivety, Minamoto Kiso Yoshinaka could have become the first Shogun of Japan.

Minamoto Yoshitsune (1159–89)

Minamoto Yoshitsune, the younger brother of Yoritomo, is one of the most famous samurai commanders in the whole of Japanese history. In spite of being short in stature and of unremarkable physique, he inspired his followers to three celebrated victories that brought the Gempei Wars to a successful conclusion for the Minamoto.

Saito Sanemori was Minamoto Yoshinaka's old retainer. At the battle of Shinowara he dyed his hair black to appear younger. Pride and honour were vitally important motivations in samurai culture.

Legend has embellished much of his life. He is said to have been taught swordfighting by the *tengu* (goblins) of the forests, and is famous for having defeated the giant monk Benkei, who became his faithful follower. Benkei was making a nuisance of himself on the Gojo Bridge in Kyoto, where he was forcibly acquiring swords from passing samurai. Young Yoshitsune defeated him in single combat. Minamoto Yoshitsune's reputation as a samurai commander, however, is much more soundly based and well deserved. He first achieved fame by the defeat of his cousin Yoshinaka in the actions described above, but it was when he was sent in pursuit of the Taira that his military genius really asserted itself.

The battle of Ichinotani in 1184 is one of his most famous victories. Ichinotani was a fortress owned by the Taira on the sea coast at Suma, to

Minamoto Kiso Yoshinaka was faithfully served by his wife (or mistress), the samurai Tomoe Gozen. Here we see her in full armour. The artist has included a *mon* (badge) of a *tomoe* (triple jewel pattern) on her armour as a pun on her name.

OPPOSITE **Minamoto Yoshitsune (1159–89) is one of the greatest names in samurai history. In this print we see him pursuing his cousin Kiso Yoshinaka at the battle of Awazu in 1184.**

the west of present-day Kobe. It was in a naturally strong position. It lay beneath steep cliffs, and the wooden walls opened on to the sea where the Taira had moored their ships. Attacks along the beach were therefore the only really practical proposition. But Minamoto Yoshitsune sent his main army along the sea coast from the west, while he led a surprise attack from the rear. This was a particularly dangerous operation, as to the rear of Ichinotani was a steep cliff with apparently no way down, but Yoshitsune led his detachment down a rough path on horseback. They stormed the rear of Ichinotani, which was relatively unguarded, and the fortress was set on fire. A fierce fight on the beach followed, and many celebrated acts of single combat took place on the sand as the Taira tried to escape to their boats. One particularly tragic incident has entered legend. A loyal follower of the Minamoto called Kumagai Naozane killed Taira Atsumori, a youth of the same age as the son he had lost. Naozane was so stricken with remorse that he gave up the warrior life and became a monk.

The majority of the Taira managed to escape by ship, and were pursued to Yashima, a volcanic plateau which in 1184 was separated from the mainland of Shikoku island by a narrow strait. The Taira lay anchored in the strait, and the Minamoto sailed across the Inland Sea by night and disembarked further along the coast. Yoshitsune's men attacked from the land, covering their movements by the smoke of burning buildings, and carried out a surprise assault similar to that at Ichinotani. Fighting continued on to the boats, and at Yashima occurred the famous incident where Yoshitsune dropped his bow into the water, and went to great pains to recover it lest the Taira realize what a comparatively weak figure he was in physical terms. His generalship, of course, belied his physique, and the Minamoto were victorious. But again the Taira escaped by sea.

Taira Tomomori (1152–85)

It may surprise the reader to find the above account of Minamoto Yoshitsune cut short at the battle of Yashima, because his greatest victory, that of Dan no Ura in 1185, had yet to happen. But the Taira had fine samurai commanders too, a state of affairs that has tended to be obscured by the fact that the Minamoto achieved the ultimate victory. This section on the Gempei Wars is concluded with a glance at the career of the man who lost at Dan no Ura, but who was nonetheless one of the finest samurai commanders of his day.

It was the leadership of Taira Tomomori, son of Taira Kiyomori, that brought about victory at the battle of Uji in 1180. With its bold attack across the river, this battle was in the finest traditions of samurai generalship. Tomomori then led an attack on the warrior monks' temple of Miidera, and effectively destroyed the potential of that place to raise

ABOVE **Minamoto Yoshitsune's most celebrated victory was the battle of Ichinotani in 1184. Yoshitsune led his detachment down a rough path on horseback. They stormed the rear of Ichinotani, which was relatively unguarded, and the fortress was set on fire. This is a splendid life-sized waxwork of the action at the Heike Monogatari Museum in Takamatsu.**

BELOW **A fierce fight on the beach followed Yoshitsune's surprise attack at Ichinotani, and many celebrated acts of single combat took place on the sand as the Taira tried to escape to their boats. A samurai has been struck by an arrow in this detail from a scroll in the Watanebe Museum, Tottori.**

an army for the remainder of the Gempei Wars. Here he was faced with a formidable army of monks behind a wall of wooden shields and felled trees.

Tomomori's brothers and cousins, however, did not share his military talents, and it is really only when Tomomori is in action that we find the Taira victorious. He achieved a notable success in 1181 at the battle of Sunomata, where the Minamoto were commanded by Yoshinaka's uncle, Minamoto Yukiie. The armies were separated by a river, which the Minamoto crossed by night in the hope of making a surprise attack. The Taira allowed them to pass within their ranks and then cut them down, identifying friend from foe because the Minamoto were dripping wet. The surviving Minamoto were forced back across the river. Retreating from Sunomata, Minamoto Yukiie attempted to make a stand by destroying the bridge over the Yahagigawa and putting up a defensive wall of shields. The Taira forced him to withdraw, but pulled back from a further pursuit when Taira Tomomori was taken ill. Tomomori also proved to be the main inspiration to his family when Yoshitsune was in the ascendant. He was present at Ichinotani and Yashima, and was instrumental in extracting the Taira from their reverses. Tomomori finally suffered defeat at the battle of Dan no Ura in 1185, the sea battle that ended the Gempei Wars. It was one of the most decisive battles in Japanese history, and the stakes were high, because the child emperor Antoku was present on one of the Taira ships.

Accounts of the battle of Dan no Ura show that the victory could have gone either way. In fact the advantage initially lay with Taira Tomomori. He was an experienced sailor, and was familiar with the local area. Yoshitsune, by contrast, had no seagoing experience and relied on various captains who had joined the Minamoto cause. Before the battle, in the words of *Heike Monogatari*, Tomomori reminded his followers that 'Even in India and China and in our own country, with the most renowned leader and the bravest warriors an army cannot prevail if fate be against it'.

The battle started with a long-range archery duel. The Taira took the initiative in the early stages because the tide was in their favour, and it appears that Taira Tomomori used his experience of the tidal conditions in the strait. At the start of the battle there was an ebb tide flowing slowly into the Inland Sea, so his ships attempted to surround the Minamoto fleet. This process took much longer than Tomomori had anticipated. By 11.00am the two fleets were closely engaged, with sword and dagger fighting taking place, but at about this time the tide changed, and began to flow westwards out of the strait. This gave the advantage to the Minamoto, who exploited it to the full. Gradually the battle turned in their favour, and victory was assured when one of the Taira commanders, Miura Yoshizumi, turned traitor and attacked the Taira from the rear. The Minamoto had assumed that the largest ship in the fleet contained the Emperor. Miura Yoshizumi revealed his true location, so the Minamoto turned their forces onto the correct target. The Minamoto archers concentrated their fire on the rowers and the helmsmen, so that the Taira ships were soon out of control, and began to drift back with the tide. Realizing that the battle was lost, many of the Taira committed suicide. Taira Tomomori was among them, and went to his death in dramatic fashion by drowning himself. According to *Heike Monogatari* he put on two suits of armour to weigh himself down, and jumped into the sea clutching his foster brother Taira Ienaga. Other accounts state that he tied an anchor to his armour and leapt into the sea. This is the version adopted in the *kabuki* dramas where Tomomori appears as either a warrior or a ghost. Taira Tomomori was without question the finest samurai commander that his illustrious yet doomed family produced, both as a leader on the battlefield and as an exemplar of the samurai virtues.

ABOVE **Minamoto Yoshitsune urges his men into the attack at the battle of Yashima in 1184. This is an excellent illustration of a samurai commander in the midst of the action.**

SAMURAI COMMANDERS OF THE 13TH CENTURY

Tomomori's defeat was also Yoshitsune's victory, but that great general did not have long to enjoy his triumph. His battles ensured that Yoritomo could become Shogun, but Yoshitsune was perceived as a rival by his brother, who forced him to flee. Yoritomo's armies hounded Yoshitsune to his death at the battle of Koromogawa in 1189.

The victorious Minamoto Yoritomo established himself as Shogun in the year 1192, and ruled from Kamakura rather than from Kyoto, the imperial capital. That once-temporary commission to make war on behalf of the emperor was made into the permanent possession of the house of Minamoto and its branches, where it stayed, with some ups and downs, for nearly eight centuries. With the ending of the Gempei Wars the notion of samurai command acquired an entirely new political meaning, and the position of Shogun grew less to represent command on the battlefield than off it. But the Minamoto Shoguns only lasted

BELOW **The Taira samurai under Taira Tomomori (1152–85), identified by the red banners, make ready to receive the attack by Minamoto Yoshitsune at the battle of Yashima in 1184.**

three generations. Following Yoritomo's death influence passed to his wife's family who manipulated the next two shoguns. The shogunate thereafter was suspended in favour of the Hojo *shikken* or Regency.

Two main challenges were mounted against the Hojo regents during the 13th century. The first was the Shokyu War, whereby Emperor Go Toba attempted to overthrow the Hojo Regency and re-establish the power of the old emperors. The Hojo army under Hojo Yasutoki left Kamakura and advanced on Kyoto, where Go Toba's army had defended the Uji bridge, just as had been done on the two previous occasions noted above. The Hojo were victorious after a long day's fighting, and crossed the bridge to enter Kyoto in triumph.

Hojo Tokimune (1251–84)

It was the Hojo who were to face the great crisis of the 13th century. This was the attempt by the Yuan (Mongol) emperor of China, Khubilai Khan, to invade Japan. When faced by the Mongol invasions, the samurai's greatest commander, Hojo Tokimune, acted as a statesman, not a general, and never wielded a sword in anger against the Mongols or anyone else. But Tokimune's presence was communicated down the chain of command to inspire scores of minor leaders to huge efforts in defence of Japan. As leader of the *shikken* it was Tokimune who received the Mongol embassies in 1268 and 1271, and his defiance in the face of Khubilai Khan's threats led to the first invasion of Japan by the Mongols in 1274. The landing took place in the vicinity of the present-day city of Fukuoka on Kyushu Island. Having ravaged the islands of Tsushima and Iki, the Mongols fought the defending samurai on Kyushu with clouds of arrows and firebombs flung by catapult. Nor did the Mongols issue challenges to worthy opponents. The unfamiliar ways of warfare caused great problems for the samurai, who faced the strange enemies with great defiance, but fortunately the invasion was called off after a day when a storm wrecked the Mongol fleet. (The Mongol retreat was probably intended to happen all along, as the Mongols routinely carried out reconnaissance in force.)

Diplomatic efforts continued over the next couple of years, but the Khan's demands were never diluted. In 1276 Tokimune ordered the execution of a Mongol ambassador and put all of western Japan on the alert for a second invasion. By the time the Mongol fleet returned

BELOW **The warrior monk Benkei accompanies Yoshitsune at the battle of Dan no Ura in 1185. Benkei was Yoshitsune's constant companion.**

BELOW RIGHT **The samurai on the boats at Dan no Ura. These flimsy craft allowed a land battle to be fought at sea.**

for a full-scale attempt in 1281, the Japanese had built a defensive wall round Hakata Bay. Horses could be ridden up an inclined slope to the rear. Here the samurai held off the attacks and then raided the vanguard of the Mongol fleet in small boats. This was perhaps the most glorious episode in the story of the invasions. When the full Mongol fleet arrived, the Japanese expected a huge attempt at landing to be made, but managed to keep the invaders at bay by hit-and-run raids. The strategy paid off, and a typhoon (called the *kami-kaze* or divine wind) blew up and smashed the Mongol ships. The survivors limped home, and no further attempt at an invasion of Japan was ever made. Sensibly, Tokimune ordered his men to fortify the coasts for several years in case of attack. The strain of defending Japan had taken a huge toll of Tokimune, and he died soon after his triumph at the young age of 34. He was mourned by all who had served him.

THE WARS BETWEEN THE COURTS

The reversed oars incident at the battle of Dan no Ura, which led Minamoto Yoshitsune to be accused of cowardice. Yoshitsune had suggested fitting oars at the front of the boats as well as the rear so that withdrawal might be made easier. Certain of his captains objected, saying that samurai always faced their enemies.

After a long period of peace, the 14th century in Japan was marked by the abortive yet long-lasting attempt by Emperor Go Daigo to reassert the power of the imperial court over that of the Shogun. Go Daigo's campaigns were of course actually conducted against the Hojo *shikken*, the institution that had temporarily supplanted the Shogun, but are nevertheless described in most accounts as being the armies of the *bakufu* or Shogunate. The resulting Nanbokucho Wars (the Wars between the Southern and Northern Courts) produced several examples of outstanding samurai commanders. It also witnessed some changes in samurai warfare, spurred on by an increase in the amount of fighting that was done on foot. Several actions involved not elite mounted archers but lower-class foot soldiers, who were given bows and discharged volleys of arrows at the opposing ranks, just as the Mongols

Samurai commanders await the arrival of the Mongols in 1281. Hojo Tokimune (1251–84), their overall commander, never drew a sword in anger but provided a statesmanlike political role.

had done. Of the 2,000 men who fought for the Sasaki at the battle of Shijo-Nawate in 1348, 800 were these lower-class archers, to whom the word *ashigaru* (light feet) was first given.

The increase in fighting on foot also led to a change in the samurai's appearance. The evidence presented by extant specimens of armour from this time indicates that the bulky, box-like suit of armour known as *yoroi* was gradually phased out in favour of a lighter, more streamlined design based on the *do-maru* (wrap around) style worn by the foot soldiers. This, like the *yoroi*, was suspended from the shoulders, but was fastened tightly around the body. To the casual eye, there seems very little difference between the two, but the new styles based on the *do-maru* acknowledged the need for armour to provide more than a passive defence for a mounted archer. As the heavy and wide skirt pieces of the *yoroi* were replaced by several smaller *kusazuri* (a style of armour-making that was to last for the rest of samurai history), the lack of solidity was compensated for by the introduction of the *haidate*, a form of thigh guard rather like an armoured apron, which was worn under the *do*. A final response to fighting on foot was the substitution of simple, disposable *waraji* (straw sandals) for the elaborate fur boots of the mounted warrior.

The samurai commander of the 14th century was therefore faced with a far more complex task than his predecessors of the Gempei Wars. Battles could take place in forests, on mountains, from stockades, and involve numerous troops. In addition there were the same grand set-piece battles that the samurai had always known, because mounted warfare was still very important in the appropriate

In the defence of Chihaya castle, Kusunoki Masashige used dummy warriors to make his forces appear larger than they were. The dummies were rigged up using straw inside spare armour.

situation. Four men stand out above all others, and it is through their careers that we see the story of the Nanbokucho Wars.

Kusunoki Masashige (1294–1336)

Kusunoki Masashige was born in 1294, and responded enthusiastically to Go Daigo's call to arms. His long service, which ended ultimately in his death, and his refusal to change sides, led to Masashige being 'discovered' as an imperial hero during the Meiji period in the late 19th century when imperial power was restored. His reputation is therefore enhanced by this association with the imperial cause.

Matters did not, however, begin well for the loyalists, and Go Daigo was speedily booted out of Kyoto by the Hojo. He fled to the nearby mountains, and the flight of Emperor Go Daigo to the mountains of Yoshino ensured that this phase of the wars developed into a long process of defending fortified camps in wooded mountainous districts. The samurai who supported Go Daigo and his descendants, who maintained his legitimacy even after the Ashikaga clan had become Shoguns and set up another emperor in Kyoto, thus fought what was largely a guerrilla war. It was conducted in the forests and mountains of central Japan, either to defend Go Daigo's person, or to harass various armies and draw them away from him. Foremost among the commanders in these operations was Kusunoki Masashige. He is best known for his loyalty unto death at the battle of Minatogawa in 1336, but that was a failure. In the mountains of Yoshino we see Masashige at his supreme best.

This new style of warfare became almost inevitable because of the great imbalance in forces between the two sides, and the process began almost as soon as Go Daigo announced his

Kusunoki Masashige (1294–1336), the greatest of the loyalist imperial commanders, as shown on a painted scroll in the Watanabe Museum, Tottori.

Kusunoki Masashige's farewell to his son. This poignant moment, when Masashige bade farewell to Masatsura, occurred just before Masashige's last battle at Minatogawa in 1336. Masatsura went on to serve the imperial cause and was killed at the battle of Shijo Nawate in 1348.

A scroll showing Masashige's use of fire in the defence of Chihaya. Boiling and flaming oil is being poured over the attacking Hojo troops.

intentions of overthrowing the *bakufu*. Remembering the fate of the previous attempt at restoration by Emperor Go Toba, which had collapsed quickly when faced with a rapid military response from Kamakura, Go Daigo and his followers fled from Kyoto, taking with them the crown jewels, and entrenched themselves on Mount Kasagi. The *bakufu* forces then had to attack a series of fortified *yamashiro* (mountain castles) on Mount Hiei and Kasagi, then the progressively stronger foundations of Akasaka and Chihaya, commanded by the great commander Kusunoki Masashige: '...the warriors within the castle threw down mighty rocks from the tower tops to smash the enemy's shields; and while the attackers were afflicted the defenders shot at them fiercely with arrows.'

These are tactics not unlike the defence of the palaces of Kyoto during the Gempei Wars, in which wooden walls protected samurai against a fierce exchange of arrows. But there are certain important differences. First, the 14th-century fighting was conducted on terrain over which mounted fighting was largely impracticable, so the horse became just a means of approaching the scene of battle, and second, the nature of the ground allowed the use of rocks, pits and booby traps as weapons. The forests are dense, and the fall of the ground quite precipitous in places. Chihaya is particularly dramatic, and must have been a death trap to an army unfamiliar with the layout of these wild and forested hills. On one occasion Kusunoki Masashige allowed the *bakufu* army to approach on horseback along the forest paths until they were quite close to the fortified line, then felled five great trees on top of them, and poured arrows down into the confused scene. On another occasion, 'when the wall was about to fall, those within the castle took ladles with handles ten or twenty feet long, collected boiling water, and poured it onto them. The hot water passed through the holes in their helmet tops, ran down from the edges of their shoulder guards, and burned their bodies so severely that they fled in terror, throwing down their shields and grapnels.'

Kusunoki Masashige fully deserves to be in the foremost rank of samurai commanders, but the loyalty for which he was renowned

26

proved to be his undoing. At the battle of Minatogawa he allowed himself to be overruled by the wishes of his emperor, and the result was a disaster for their cause. As long as he was in command, Kusunoki Masashige remained undefeated. It was only when the ultimate decision for campaigning was taken from him that he was to be tragically defeated in that episode which is related below under the name of the general who won, Ashikaga Takauji.

Nitta Yoshisada (1301–38)

Nitta Yoshisada, another samurai commander who was to make a name for himself as an imperial loyalist during the Nanbokucho Wars, served first in the *bakufu* army against Kusunoki Masashige, but changed sides. His first target after this, in 1333, was the *bakufu*'s capital of Kamakura, which provided a very different challenge to his leadership from the forest warfare of Chihaya. Kamakura was defended on three sides by mountains and on the fourth by the sea. Nitta Yoshisada divided his forces into three divisions to attack from the north, east and west. In spite of hours of fierce fighting, no real breakthrough could be achieved by the

Nitta Yoshisada (1301–38) at Kamakura in 1333. This was the moment when Yoshisada threw his sword into the sea as an offering to the Sun Goddess.

loyalists, particularly on the western side, where the Gokurakuji Pass was held firmly behind rows of stout wooden shields. Nitta Yoshisada went there himself to take a closer look, and realized that there was a chance of by-passing Gokurakuji altogether if it were possible to round the cape where the promontory of Inamuragasaki projects into the sea. There was a small expanse of beach at low tide, but the tide was then high, and the Hojo had taken the added precaution of placing several ships a short distance from the shore, from which a barrage of arrows could cover any flanking attack. At this point there occurred the great legend of the battle of Kamakura: when Nitta Yoshisada threw his sword into the sea as an offering to the Sun Goddess, the waters parted to let his army through.

Once Nitta Yoshisada's troops were in the city the battle became a fierce hand-to-hand struggle among the burning houses. The Hojo forces were torn between holding the passes and resisting the new advance around the cape, but when the battle was seen to be lost, the Hojo family and their closest retainers decided to die like true samurai and committed an act of mass suicide.

Nitta Yoshisada stayed loyal to Go Daigo when Ashikaga Takauji revolted against him. Yoshisada defeated Takauji at Yahagigawa and in Suruga province, but was defeated in turn at Hakone. It was Nitta Yoshisada who was responsible for Ashikaga Takauji's flight to Kyushu. The taking of Kamakura was nonetheless Nitta Yoshisada's greatest triumph, but his final campaign saw him being despatched by Go Daigo to capture the fortress of Fujishima, an ordinary wooden stockade enclosure defended by warrior monks. Yoshisada was surprised by the determined resistance put up by the monks of Fujishima. Realizing that he would have to take the lead if his men were to break through, Yoshisada led the way through the rice fields, where the enemy's foot soldiers had erected wooden shields and began to loose hundreds of arrows at him. Yoshisada's mounted attendants tried to form a line in front of him to protect him from the archery, but one by one they were struck down and killed. An arrow then smashed through Yoshisada's helmet and into his forehead. Still conscious, Yoshisada committed

Nitta Yoshisada is killed at the battle of Fujishima.

suicide, but not by *hara-kiri*. There was no time for that, nor did his trapped position allow him to reach his abdomen. Instead Nitta Yoshisada is said to have cut off his own head. It rolled into a rice paddy and his body slid in after it. To cut off one's own head sounds far fetched, but in the heat of the battle and with a samurai sword of legendary sharpness it is entirely believable for someone with Yoshisada's fanaticism and in such desperate straits.

Nitta Yoshisada is regarded as second only to Kusunoki Masashige in his loyalty to the emperor, but his skills as a general were by no means on a par. There is no doubt that he was a great fighting man, but he never quite regained the winning form he had had at Kamakura.

Ashikaga Takauji (1305–58)

Because of his loyalty to the emperor, Nitta Yoshisada is revered as a paragon of samurai virtue along with Kusunoki Masashige. This is of course to forget the fact that he initially opposed Go Daigo, as did the third samurai commander in this section: Ashikaga Takauji. In both political and military terms his achievements were far greater than either Masashige's or Yoshisada's, but the fact that he first opposed Go Daigo, then supported him, and finally abandoned him, coupled with his presumption to die 'with his boots off', meant that he never became a samurai hero.

Ashikaga Takauji was born in 1305. We first hear of him in action when the *bakufu* ordered him to attack Kusunoki Masashige's fortress at Kasagi in 1331. Two years later he declared for the emperor and, while Nitta Yoshisada was completing the ruin of the Hojo in Kamakura, Takauji was performing a similar operation in Kyoto where he destroyed the Hojo headquarters at Rokuhara. Because of Takauji, therefore, more than anyone else, Go Daigo was able to return to the imperial capital and claim his throne. It was then that things started to go wrong. Takauji did not feel that he had been adequately rewarded for his services, and as the Ashikaga were descended from Minamoto stock he alone among Go Daigo's supporters could aspire to the dignity of Shogun. The opportunity presented itself when elements among the surviving Hojo re-occupied the ruins of Kamakura. Takauji headed east of his own accord 'for the good of the realm' as he put it. He ousted the Hojo, and waited in Kamakura to see whether he would be rewarded or punished. Go Daigo's response was to send an army against Takauji under Nitta Yoshisada, which defeated Takauji's vanguard. But Takauji's support never wavered, and when he had gathered allies about him he headed back for Kyoto, forcing Go Daigo to flee once again. The imperialist reaction to this was swift, and soon Takauji was ousted from Kyoto by Nitta Yoshisada and sent fleeing from the main island of Honshu to the southern island of Kyushu.

Putting on armour. The samurai shown here are the subordinate 'Twenty-Four Generals' of the Takeda family.

Samurai with cherry blossom. No more meaningful symbol for the samurai exists than the cherry blossom, which flowers for such a short time.

Ashikaga Takauji's subsequent triumphant return from military exile in Kyushu is one of the most remarkable reversals of fortune in Japanese history. At the battle of Tatarahama his forces defeated Kikuchi Taketoshi. With this victory Takauji gained sufficient support to be able to return to Honshu. He was challenged at the battle of Minatogawa, fought where the city of Kobe now stands. The battle is famous for the loyalty displayed by Kusunoki Masashige, who was in favour of withdrawing to the mountains to fight a guerrilla war. Emperor Go Daigo wanted to make a stand against the Ashikaga, and Kusunoki's sense of duty forced him to agree, although he knew the situation was hopeless. Ashikaga Takauji advanced by ship along the coast of the Inland Sea, while his brother Ashikaga Tadayoshi, whose vanguard was led by Shoni Yorihisa, advanced by land. They were joined by a large seaborne reinforcement from Shikoku led by the Hosokawa, who tried to land but were driven off and forced to land further along the coast. When the battle started, Nitta Yoshisada was attacked by the Shoni family's troops and was forced back, leaving Kusunoki Masashige dangerously isolated. Masashige was soon totally surrounded, and committed suicide as his army collapsed.

Ashikaga Takauji re-entered Kyoto and declared that Go Daigo had forfeited his throne. In his place Takauji set up his own nominee as emperor. This was the beginning of a schism between the Ashikaga's Northern Emperors and the fugitive Southern Emperors. In 1338 the Northern Emperor made Ashikaga Takauji Shogun. His descendants, the Ashikaga dynasty, were to enjoy power for two centuries. Takauji's achievements were therefore quite remarkable. He captured Kyoto from the Hojo, and finally secured Kamakura after Nitta's famous victory. His triumph at Minatogawa was a masterpiece of tactics, and he set in place a dynasty that lasted almost as long as the Tokugawa. His generalship and leadership were both superb, and by the time he died from cancer in 1358 he had established himself as the outstanding samurai commander of the War between the Courts.

Ashikaga Yoshimitsu (1358–1408)

The Wars between the Courts dragged on for another half century after the death of Ashikaga Takauji, and were resolved only because of the efforts of one of the most remarkable characters in Japanese history. Yoshimitsu was the third Ashikaga Shogun, and is best known for his role as a statesman and for being the builder of the Kinkakuji, the 'Temple of the Golden Pavilion', in Kyoto. But these achievements occurred after he had retired from active political life. During his reign as Shogun he showed himself to be an astute politician as well as a fine samurai commander, even if the latter role has been hitherto unrecognized.

Yoshimitsu became Shogun in 1367. The steady progress of the War between the Courts meant that by 1374 the supporters of the Southern Court were in defeat and disarray almost everywhere in Japan. Kyushu remained an exception, and when Imagawa Sadayo, despatched by Yoshimitsu to settle the matter, failed in his duties, the young Shogun led a further expedition in person that was entirely successful. On returning to Kyoto, Yoshimitsu carried out programmes that raised the prestige of the Ashikaga *bakufu* to its highest level. Embassies were set up with Ming China and trade with China was encouraged, a matter in which Yoshimitsu was very fortunate, for the Yuan (Mongol) dynasty had recently been overthrown and replaced by the Ming. The time was therefore opportune to repair the damage that had been caused to Sino-Japanese relations by the Mongol invasions. Yoshimitsu also took a strong line on the matter of the Japanese pirates who had been raiding the coastline of Korea and China.

Yet even Yoshimitsu was not without rivals. The Yamana clan in particular had grown strong through the petty conflicts that characterised the last years of the Wars between the Courts. Two brothers, Yamana Yoshimasa and Yamana Ujikiyo, had briefly opposed the Shogun only to be defeated in battle, and then their nephew Yamana Mitsuyuki launched a much more serious attempt in 1391. The Yamana attacked Kyoto, but Yoshimitsu routed the army and distributed much of the domains of the family among his own generals, leaving the Yamana with only two provinces. It was a victory that gave Yoshimitsu great confidence and made the position of the Shogun look virtually unassailable, so Yoshimitsu seized the moment to bring the imperial schism to an end. The Southern Emperor, Go Kameyama, was persuaded to submit, and transferred the imperial regalia to Go Komatsu, the Emperor of the North. There would still be sporadic risings in the name of successive heirs to the Southern Court over the next half century, but none lasted long, and Yoshimitsu deserves the credit as the man who brought reconciliation and peace to Japan.

Ashikaga Yoshimitsu was to face one final military challenge during his glorious reign. Ouchi Yoshihiro (1356–1400) had been one of Yoshimitsu's staunchest supporters, serving in Kyushu in 1374, helping in the defence of Kyoto against Yamana Mitsuyuki in 1391, and then conducting the negotiations that brought about the end of the imperial schism. But in 1399 he responded to the advances of a rival member of the Ashikaga family who thought he should be Shogun. It was the first major military campaign in Japan after the end of the Nanbokucho Wars. Yoshihiro's strength lay in western Japan, where he had close links with the pirate fleets of the Inland Sea. Ouchi Yoshihiro planned his campaign carefully, safeguarding his rear by alliances and seeking reinforcements from discontented warriors in the area of the capital. Among them was his former enemy Yamana Mitsuyuki. Yoshihiro marched east and joined Mitsuyuki at the town of Sakai, near present-day Osaka. He fortified the town with wooden walls and towers, and sank wells in case of a siege.

Yoshimitsu first opened negotiations with the rebel, but when these failed he led a military advance in person. Sakai was a port town, so while Yoshimitsu led three attacks from the landward side some pirates in the pay of the *bakufu* sought to cut the lines of communication with the

Inland Sea. The assault stalled at the defences Yoshihiro had erected, and for some weeks the fighting was indecisive and settled down to become a siege. But in the middle of January 1400 a strong north wind was blowing, so the *bakufu* used that most deadly of samurai weapons – fire, that quickly spread through the town. Yoshihiro's central fortress soon caught alight, and then assaults from every side crushed his rebel army. Yoshihiro committed suicide on the field of battle.

The essence of Ashikaga Yoshimitsu's personal achievements lay in great events like the reconciliation between the rival emperors, but through actions like the Kyushu campaign and the siege of Sakai he showed that he was also a fine commander of samurai. In this book we have seen Yoritomo the statesman and Yoshitsune the warrior, but none compare to Ashikaga Yoshimitsu, who combined almost every role that a Shogun could have – politician, warrior and aesthete – in one consummate individual. He died suddenly from illness in 1408 at the still vigorous age of 50, having made a unique personal contribution to Japanese history.

THE ONIN WAR

When Yamana Mitsuyuki committed suicide at the siege of Sakai in 1400, the ruin of his family looked complete. Few would have guessed that within two more generations the name of Yamana was to be associated with one of the pivotal events in Japanese history, the Onin War, in which Mitsuyuki's great-nephew, Mochitoyo, was one of the two main protagonists. The Onin War was the conflict, or rather series of conflicts, that marked the beginning of the Sengoku Jidai, 'the period of warring states', an expression taken from a similarly anarchic period in ancient Chinese history. The Onin War has one other feature that marks it off from other conflicts. By 1467 the presence of the *bakufu* headquarters had encouraged most of the important samurai to maintain residences within a small area of northern Kyoto. This graceful district was to become the most bizarre and unwelcome battlefield in samurai history.

Yamana Sozen Mochitoyo (1404–73) and Hosokawa Katsumoto (1430–73)

The commanders of the rival sides in the Onin War must be treated as a pair. The leader of the Yamana, Mochitoyo, was an excessively ambitious leader of men. He had been born in 1404, and inherited the domains of his father in 1435. Mochitoyo became a Buddhist monk in 1441, taking the name of Sozen. His excessive rages, which drove him near to fits, earned him the nickname of the 'Red Monk', for during such attacks his face became bright red. His enemy in

The display of a severed head before one's commander was the best proof of duty done. This bizarre ritual was vitally important, and after a battle a samurai commander would sit in state to examine the trophies.

(continued on page 41)

EARLY SAMURAI COMMANDERS
1: Taira Masakado (c.903–40)
2: Minamoto Yoriyoshi (995–1082)
3: Minamoto Kiso Yoshinaka (1154–84)

SAMURAI COMMANDERS OF THE GEMPEI WARS
1: Taira Tomomori (1152–85)
2: Minamoto Yoshitsune (1159–89)

B

THE LOYALIST COMMANDERS
1: Kusunoki Masashige (1294–1336)
2: Nitta Yoshisada (1301–38)

C

ASHIKAGA TAKAUJI (1305–58)

D

SAMURAI COMMANDERS OF THE ONIN WAR
1: Yamana Sozen Mochitoyo (1404–73)
2: Hosokawa Katsumoto (1430–73)

E

SAMURAI COMMANDERS OF THE
EARLY SENGOKU PERIOD
1: Hojo Soun (1432–1519)
2: Togashi Masachika (died 1488)

F

SHIMAZU TAKAHISA (1514–71)

THE FOURTH BATTLE OF
KAWANAKAJIMA
1: Takeda Shingen (1521–73)
2: Uesugi Kenshin (1530–78)

H

the Onin War, Hosokawa Katsumoto, was his son-in-law. Katsumoto, born in 1430, was of a character diametrically opposite to that of his tempestuous father-in-law. While the Red Monk raged Hosokawa kept a calm disposition.

For a number of years prior to the Onin War, the two rivals had been interfering in the affairs of other families. There was a succession dispute in the Hatakeyama family in 1450, and soon after one in the Shiba family. Sozen made as much political capital as he could out of the situations, hoping thereby to gain allies for the eventual showdown with the Hosokawa. Eventually there came an ideal excuse for a dispute. The Shogun, Ashikaga Yoshimasa, expressed a desire to abdicate. He had no son to whom he could pass the Shogunate, so he brought out his brother Yoshimi from a monastery. Unfortunately, a year later Yoshimasa's wife gave birth to a son. Yamana Sozen offered his support for the cause of the infant Yoshihisa, while Hosokawa Katsumoto pledged his loyalty to the brother Yoshimi. The two rivals had now arranged themselves on opposite sides in a dispute concerning the highest office in the land.

Both Yamana and Hosokawa realized that their long-awaited conflict was nigh, so they summoned the forces at their disposal. It soon became clear that the battlefield was to be the city of Kyoto itself, as both sides looked around for suitable houses to use as headquarters and studied the strategic position of the northern streets. At the end of February 1467, the mansion of one of Hosokawa's generals mysteriously went up in flames. In April Hosokawa samurai attacked a group of Sozen's troops bringing rice into the city. The crisis was imminent, and all the citizens who could flee began evacuating the city. The younger members of the imperial family were moved out for safety, and the guard on the palace was doubled as rumours of impending attacks flew about.

The Onin War officially began at the end of May 1467, when the Hosokawa attacked the mansion of Isshiki. Some indication of the ruin to come was given as the attack spread. In the wake of the fighting came the looting and burning; soon the whole block containing the Isshiki mansion was burnt out. For the next month similar raids and attacks continued so that by the beginning of July much of northern Kyoto had been reduced to rubble and ashes. Barricades had been built across the streets, and as the houses disappeared the defences were augmented by trenches.

Meanwhile, Yamana Sozen had received reinforcements and at the end of October attacked the monastery of Shokoku-ji. Fighting went on among the hot ashes until night fell and both sides retired exhausted. The carnage had been dreadful, and the narrow streets were choked with corpses; eight carts were later filled with the heads of the slain. During the first few months of 1468 the fighting abated somewhat, and settled down to the tedium of what was virtually trench warfare, as the two sides glared at each other from barricades and prepared positions. The Hosokawa brought up traction trebuchets and bombarded the Yamana positions with stones and exploding bombs. No man's land was an expanse of blackened timbers being slowly buried under a growth of weeds, divided in two by a trench 20ft wide and 10ft deep.

As stalemate settled upon Kyoto, the fighting spread to the provinces, the samurai leaders outside the capital having been encouraged by the dramatic demonstration of the breakdown of *bakufu* power. The campaigns directly associated with the Onin War are reckoned to have lasted until 1476, by which time Japan had entered the chaos of the Sengoku period. But Yamana Sozen and Hosokawa Katsumoto, who had started the process, were now both dead. Sozen died, exhausted, in his 70th year, while his nephew followed him suddenly two months later. Katsumoto was only 44 and his death unexpected.

Togashi Masachika (died 1488)

The pattern of alliances that grew out of the rivalries of the Onin War yields a further example of a successful samurai commander of the 15th century. In some ways Togashi Masachika is typical of his times. He fought to secure his inheritance and headed off serious challenges as he built up a domain using his skills in leading samurai into battle. Where he differs from the rest is in the manner of his final defeat. Togashi Masachika eventually lost his territories not to rival samurai but to a peasant army, thus providing a dreadful example to every other *daimyo* in Japan.

The Togashi family could trace their origins back to the 12th century, but they achieved prominence only when Togashi Takaie became one of the earliest supporters of Ashikaga Takauji in 1336. His reward was to be made *shugo* (Shogun's deputy) of Kaga province in 1336. During the century that followed, the Togashi succeeded in building up a strong vassal organization – the key to any victory on the battlefield – but by the 1440s the system had begun to break down. The result was the division of the province between two vassal factions. Togashi Masachika was forced to live in genteel exile in Kyoto, where he still bore the nominal title of *shugo* of Kaga.

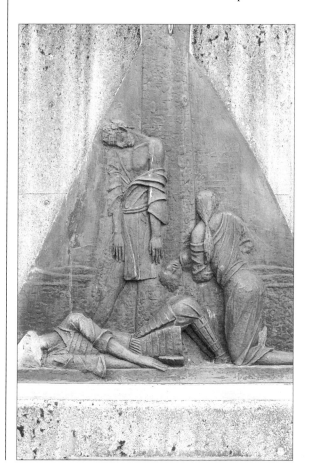

The monument to the Ikko-ikki at Torigoe. These were the men who deposed Togashi Masachika and produced a province run by peasants for a century. They were eventually overcome by the generals of Oda Nobunaga.

When the Onin War began in 1467 Masachika became involved on the side of Hosokawa Katsumoto. The vassals who controlled southern Kaga still regarded Masachika as *shugo*, but their rivals in the northern half of the province recognized his younger brother Kochiyo. They naturally took the part of the rival Yamana in the Onin War and, equally as naturally, invaded southern Kaga when the opportunity presented itself. Togashi Masachika was now cut off completely from his province, but when Asakura Toshikage of Echizen province changed sides from Yamana to Hosokawa in 1471, Masachika found himself with a new ally. Echizen, which bordered Kaga, would also be a good jumping-off point for reconquest.

Togashi Masachika's main problem now was to find allies in Kaga itself. He did not have far to look, even if the choice he was presented with was a little unusual for a samurai commander. Echizen and Kaga were hotbeds of the Ikko-ikki, the militant Buddhist organization that had arisen out of the Jodo-Shinshu, the True Pure Land sect. Shinshu followers placed all their faith in the saving power of Amida Buddha, reciting his name in a simple invocation called *nembutsu,* 'Buddha calling'. Jodo-Shinshu, the largest Buddhist sect in modern Japan, owed its growth in the 15th century to the preaching of the revivalist Rennyo, who had settled on the sea coast of Echizen province at a place called Yoshizaki. Within two years a town consisting of 100 houses had grown up around it.

These were the men that Togashi Masachika sought to enlist for his own ends. He made extravagant promises concerning the rewards that would be available should they assist him in regaining his province, but his brother Kochiyo got to hear of the plot. In 1474 Kochiyo launched a pre-emptive strike against Yoshizaki. The Ikko-ikki *monto* (followers) erected hasty defences of sharpened stakes and vowed to fight to the death. Their pacifist leader Rennyo urged them not to resist, but when the Togashi samurai moved into the attack, the Ikko-ikki responded with a fanaticism born of a belief that death in battle meant an instant entrance into the Pure Land. A bloody battle ensued, producing 2,000 dead among the *monto*. But they drove Kochiyo off, and followed up their victory by attacking his castle at Rendaiji. Kochiyo was defeated, and Masachika gained his inheritance, rejoicing at the evidence of how well the Ikko-ikki had done his work of conquest for him.

But, as in so many cases in samurai history, the rewards promised before a campaign did not fully materialize after it. So the Ikko-ikki rebelled. But Masachika was ready for them, and demonstrated his newly won authority by a sound military defeat and severe persecution. The Ikko-ikki *monto* were forced to flee north to Etchu province, from where they sent messages to Rennyo in Echizen, asking him to intercede on their behalf with Masachika. Shimotsuma Rensu, a samurai supporter of the Ikko-ikki and a close personal adviser to Rennyo, took it upon himself to issue a call to arms in Rennyo's name. The proclamation urged all the *monto* in Kaga to rise against Togashi Masachika. The resulting insurgency happened in the sixth month of 1474 and was a complete failure. However, Masachika was a generous victor. The sect was not banned and the members were allowed to return home.

Over the next few years Togashi Masachika consolidated his position in Kaga. It was no easy task, because the Ikko-ikki were restless and, when the chance came to ingratiate himself in the eyes of the Shogun, Masachika responded enthusiastically, hoping that a successful campaign on the Shogun's behalf would yield military assistance in Kaga. But the task required of him was to quell a rebel samurai leader, Rokkaku Takayori, in distant Omi province. It was almost a suicide mission, and Masachika was the only distant *shugo* to respond positively.

Needless to say, the Ikko-ikki took advantage of the absence of Masachika and in the 12th month of 1487 their army attacked Masachika's weakly defended castle. Masachika rushed back from Omi. He had some initial successes, but a number of Togashi vassals joined in the rebellion and named Masachika's uncle as an alternative *shugo*. In 1488, the Ikko-ikki of Yoshizaki again attacked Togashi Masachika's Tako castle with an army said to have numbered 200,000 men. Faced with certain defeat, Masachika committed suicide in the flames of his burning castle. The Ikko-ikki took over the province and, in a unique demonstration of 'people power', were to rule Kaga for the next 100 years, consigning Masachika to a place in history as being the successful samurai commander who finally lost to what was virtually a peasant army.

SAMURAI COMMANDERS IN THE EARLY SENGOKU PERIOD

The breakdown of central authority led to the growth of the *daimyo*, whose local authority in the provinces owed nothing to the favour of a Shogun. Some were from well-established military houses. Many were highly skilled military opportunists. Such daimyo seized power by usurpation, by murder, by waging war or by marriage contracts to influential neighbours – indeed by any means that would safeguard their positions and their livelihoods. The physical evidence of this trend started appearing on top of hundreds of Japanese mountains in the form of *yamashiro*. From chains of these simple fortresses particular *daimyo* controlled and guarded their provinces against optimistic tax collectors and pessimistic rivals.

The smaller scale samurai commanders needed fighting men, and could not summon the large numbers that had previously been easy for large landowners like Yamana Sozen. So for a landless peasant who was handy with a sword and dissatisfied with his lot, the lawlessness of the times offered a sellers' market, and it is at this time that we more and more frequently come across *ashigaru* (foot soldiers, literally 'light feet'), the name indicating their lack of armour, footwear or even weaponry until all three could be looted from a defeated enemy. These *ashigaru* found it easy to attach themselves casually to samurai armies, and then fight, pillage and ultimately desert.

As time went by, the more astute *daimyo* came to several conclusions concerning the *ashigaru* in their service. While some continued to accept into their armies a loose and uncertain rabble, others began to ask questions about both quantity and quality, and the first conclusion was that men casually recruited could just as casually disappear to till the fields and swell the armies of an enemy. The second point was an appreciation that the use of an unorganized band of untrained peasants attracted only by personal gain was not conducive to the need to fight in disciplined groups and wield increasingly sophisticated weapons. There was therefore a need for continuity, for development of skills, and above all for the inculcation of at least a little of that fanatical loyalty that was already expected from the samurai. Both these trends developed as the Sengoku period continued, with battles, sieges and campaigns growing larger in scale. The final conclusion was a recognition that, although the *ashigaru* were different from samurai, their fighting skills could be complementary. In other words, the successful samurai commander of the Sengoku period was one who took *ashigaru* seriously, and used them in a combination of arms, controlled, trained and drilled by samurai, but recognized and valued for the contribution they could make in the achievement of victory.

This practice of using foot solders as missile troops, and the additional growing trend towards large armies, resulted in the most important change in cavalry tactics in the whole of samurai history. Somehow the samurai horseman had to hit back, needing to use his mobility and striking power to provide the shock of a charge against the opposing *ashigaru*. The problem was that a samurai carried a bow, which was an encumbrance in hand-to-hand fighting, and even if the bow was given to an attendant, swords were of limited use from the saddle. So, in a dramatic change to established practice, the bow was abandoned in favour of the spear, and the mounted archer gave way to the mounted spearman. Some mounted archers were still retained, operating as mobile sharpshooters, but the majority of samurai now carried spears fitted with blades that were every bit as sharp as their swords. Some samurai preferred short spear blades, while others liked long ones. Some spears were fitted with crossblades to pull an opponent from his saddle, but all would be protected from the weather when not in use by a lacquered wooden scabbard. *Yabusame* was replaced by spear techniques from the saddle, and for the first time in Japanese history a samurai army could deliver something that could be recognized as a cavalry charge.

This pattern of warfare was to continue up to the time when firearms became common in samurai armies. The biographies of the samurai commanders that follow cover their careers prior to this important innovation, although in some cases their lives spanned that great transition.

Hojo Soun (1432–1519), the founder of the Odawara Hojo, from a hanging scroll showing him as a monk.

Hojo Soun (1432–1519)

Hojo Soun is probably the best example of a samurai commander in the early part of the Sengoku period. In 1480 Ise Shinkuro Nagauji, as he was then called, had only six men under his command. By the time of the death of his great-great grandson in 1590 that original war band had grown to tens of thousands, who defended their territory from formidable castles. Hojo Soun has often been portrayed as a very lowly samurai, or even a *ronin* (a warrior unemployed because of the death or disgrace of his master), but in fact Soun had very respectable family connections. He was born in 1432, and his elder sister had married Imagawa Yoshitada from that illustrious family in Suruga province. When Yoshitada was killed in battle in 1480 his son Ujichika's rightful inheritance was placed in great peril, so Ise Shinkuro went to his assistance with the above-mentioned six men. His military skills settled the matter, for which he received the reward of a castle from the grateful heir. In 1493 Ise Soun, who had adopted the name Soun upon becoming a monk, was provided with a further opportunity to right wrongs and do well out of it. A certain Chachamaru, a young man who had not yet received his adult name and was the nephew of the Shogun Yoshimasa, was dispossessed and ordered by his father to enter

Hojo Soun begins the invasion of Izu province. Here he is in a martial vein, with a full suit of armour and a monk's cowl. Supplies are being loaded from boats.

a monastery. Chachamaru responded by murdering his stepmother and brother-in-law, so the ever-helpful Soun went to war and destroyed Chachamaru. With the support of those who had welcomed the move, Soun added the Ashikaga's Izu province to his own territories.

The following year, Soun acquired for the Hojo the site that was to be the family's future capital: Odawara on Sagami Bay. The story of Soun's capture of Odawara is somewhat un-savoury but not untypical of the age, because he allegedly arranged for the castle's young lord to be murdered while out hunting. In 1512 Kamakura, the ancient shogunal capital, was also added to the Hojo terri-tories, followed by Arai castle in 1518, famous for the defiant suicide of the defeated lord Miura Yoshi-moto, who cut off his own head. Soun's subsequent change of name from Ise to Hojo was done to associate his new and powerful family in this part of Japan with the earlier Hojo of Kamakura, who had ruled Japan as regents for 150 years. It was the Kamakura Hojo who had repelled the Mongol invasions. The new Hojo (who are often called the Odawara Hojo) also helped themselves to the Kamakura Hojo's *mon* (heraldic badge). Hojo Soun died the following year at the age of 88, renowned not only as a warrior but as a skilful administrator. He left his son a code of laws that became a model for *daimyo* rule.

Hojo Ujitsuna (1487–1541)

Hojo Soun was succeeded by his son Hojo Ujitsuna, who continued his father's programme of conquest. In 1524 Ujitsuna led an army against Edo castle, which lay in the centre of the important rice-growing area of the Kanto plain. Edo castle is now the Imperial Palace in Tokyo, but at that time it was an ordinary castle guarding a fishing village, and its owner, Uesugi Tomooki, was most reluctant to give it up to the Hojo. In fact Tomooki took the initiative by marching his troops out to stop the Hojo advance at an important river crossing called Takanawa, but Hojo

Ujitsuna cleverly by-passed him and assaulted the Uesugi from the rear. Tomooki then retreated back to Edo, only to find that the castle-keeper, Ota Suketada, was in secret communication with the Hojo and had opened the gates to them.

The loss of Edo to the Hojo set in motion 17 years of war between the Uesugi and the Hojo for control of the Kanto, and the initiative continued to swing from one side to the other and back again. In 1526 Uesugi's ally Satomi Sanetaka scored a notable triumph over the Hojo when he captured Kamakura from them and burned to the ground the great Tsurugaoka Hachiman shrine. Soon the Hojo had rivals on their western flank as well, because when Imagawa Yoshimoto succeeded to the headship of the Imagawa in Suruga province, he turned his back on the service once provided to his ancestors by Soun, and made an alliance with the Takeda against the Hojo.

The Uesugi came back into the fray in 1535 when Tomooki noticed the absence of Hojo Ujitsuna from his home province (he was busy fighting the Takeda) and invaded Hojo territories. But Ujitsuna managed to return in time, and defeated the Uesugi at Iruma. Tomooki died in his castle of Kawagoe in 1537 and was succeeded by Uesugi Tomosada. Guessing that the Uesugi would be in some disarray, Hojo Ujitsuna attacked and captured Kawagoe, and the Hojo finally had the key to the Kanto.

Hojo Soun leads his men into battle. Waving his war fan, the traditional symbol of command for a general, Soun leads an attack.

Hojo Ujitsuna (1487–1541), the second generation of the Hojo dynasty and the victor of the battle of Konodai in 1537.

Shimosa province, which lay just round Tokyo Bay, was their next objective. Opposing the Hojo in 1537 was an allied army of Ashikaga Yoshiaki and Satomi Yoshitaka, who was based at his castle of Konodai. Ashikaga Yoshiaki was advised by his allies to attack the Hojo before they had a chance to cross the Tonegawa River towards them. The over-confident Yoshiaki, however, refused to move, but it soon became obvious that the Hojo were driving his men back. Satomi Yoshitaka then descended from Konodai hill along with Yoshiaki's eldest son, Motoyori. With his comrades being killed all around him, Motoyori stood steadfast and killed 30 of the Hojo samurai until being overcome himself. When news of the death of his son reached Yoshiaki he went mad with rage. An archer from the Hojo ranks recognized him and put a shaft into his chest. With his death the advantage immediately returned to the Hojo side, and the castle of Konodai was theirs.

By the time he died in 1541, Hojo Ujitsuna had completed the rebuilding of Kamakura, making it, together with Odawara and Edo, into a symbol of the growing power of the Hojo. Many samurai came from other parts of Japan to settle in the Hojo domains, the greatest compliment that any *daimyo* could have received.

Hojo Ujiyasu (1515–70)

The third generation was represented by Hojo Ujiyasu, who is generally regarded as the finest of the five Hojo *daimyo*. When Uesugi Tomosada heard of the death of Ujitsuna he tried unsuccessfully to recapture Edo castle. In 1545 Tomosada allied himself with Ashikaga Haruuji and marched against Kawagoe castle, which was defended by Ujiyasu's brother, Hojo Tsunanari. Tsunanari's garrison was only 3,000 strong, but it managed to hold out against 85,000 besiegers. Hojo Ujiyasu marched to Kawagoe's relief with 8,000 soldiers, sending a message carried by a brave samurai through the Uesugi siege lines to let his brother know that help was on the way. The relief force was another pitifully small army, but so confident was Ujiyasu that he decided to make a night attack. The plans worked perfectly and, outnumbered by eight to one, the Hojo triumphed. The coalition against them was utterly destroyed, and the Hojo control of the Kanto was dramatically confirmed. Hojo Ujiyasu also fought off a siege of Odawara in 1560 and one of Edo castle in 1563. He was also exceedingly active on the political front, making marriage alliances and courting support from other *daimyo*. It was Ujiyasu who raised the power of the Odawara Hojo to their greatest height, and when he died of illness in 1570 he left seven sons to continue his work.

Hojo Ujiyasu, the third Hojo *daimyo* and the greatest of his line. He was the contemporary of Takeda Shingen and Uesugi Kenshin.

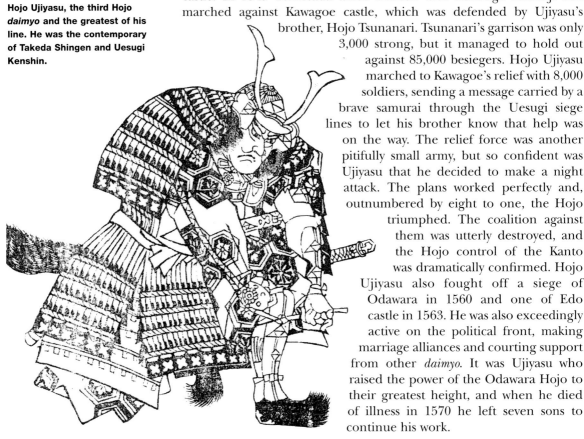

Mori Motonari (1497–1571)

Mori Motonari was a *daimyo* of the Inland Sea area who led his family to greatness, largely at the expense of the Ouchi, whose retainer he was. Tiring of war, Ouchi Yoshitaka indulged more and more in pleasures until he was deposed by his retainer, Sue Harukata. Mori Motonari's destruction of Sue Harukata is one of the most colourful episodes in samurai history.

Sue Harukata had fortified the holy island of Miyajima in the Inland Sea. Taking advantage of a blinding rainstorm, the Mori launched a surprise attack in 1555. Mori Motonari and his two sons, Mori Takamoto and Kikkawa Motoharu, sailed round the northern tip of the island to land unseen on a beach to the rear of the Sue positions. At the same time Mori's other son, Kobayakawa Takakage, sailed up the strait in full view of the Sue castle, just to put the defenders off the scent. When he was out of sight he doubled back and made a frontal assault at dawn. This was synchronised with his father's attack from the rear. It was a mark of Motonari's tactical genius that he was able to co-ordinate two amphibious landings, and the resounding victory was much deserved. By the victory of Miyajima the Mori were raised to a pre-eminent position in this part of Japan. Motonari captured Yamaguchi in 1557, but his most unusual claim to fame is that he personally met the expenses of the enthronement ceremonies of Emperor Ogimachi. Motonari died in 1571 as the lord of ten provinces.

Mori Motonari (1497–1571), the samurai commander whose naval skill helped his family to dominate the area of the Inland Sea.

Shimazu Takahisa (1514–71)

To some extent Shimazu Takahisa represents a transitional stage between the old *daimyo* and the new. For centuries the ancient Shimazu family lay outside the mainstream of Japanese political life and kept their position as local rulers in spite of all the upsets of the Onin War. This was largely due to their geographical position, because the three provinces they owned were Satsuma, Osumi and Hyuga, at the furthest tip of the southern island of Kyushu. All this was to change during the reign of the 15th Shimazu *daimyo*, Takahisa. In 1543 some Portuguese traders were shipwrecked on the island of Tanegashima in Shimazu territory. They brought with them European arquebuses, the first ever seen in Japan, and within months the swordsmiths of Satsuma had become gunsmiths. In 1549 Shimazu Takahisa became the first samurai commander to use such weapons in battle when he captured Kajiki castle. In that same year he entertained the Jesuit Francis Xavier when the latter arrived for the first Christian missionary enterprise in Japan.

Takahisa was no less successful in battle. He was supported by three fine young sons who were to inherit his domains, and a core of fanatically loyal retainers. Over the next few years the Shimazu territory gradually expanded by the capture of other fortresses on their borders. In 1554 Takahisa led his men to victory when they captured Iwatsurugi castle. This

Shimazu Takahisa, shown here as a monk, was the first of the great family of commanders from southern Japan.

was a *yamashiro,* approachable only by steep and narrow paths, up which the Shimazu samurai made their way. In 1555 he took Chosahira castle, and in 1556 Matsuzaka, thus giving the Shimazu a series of strongpoints to the north of Satsuma. Shimazu Takahisa, who died of illness in 1571, was a far-sighted ruler. His military campaigns may have been limited in their objectives, but they were fundamental in laying the foundations for the major conflicts in which his sons Yoshihisa and Yoshihiro would shortly become involved. They would take the Shimazu to the very heights of their greatness.

Imagawa Yoshimoto (1519–60)

Imagawa Yoshimoto is best known to history for being the loser at the battle of Okehazama in 1560, the conflict from which the reunification of Japan is traditionally seen as beginning. But this is to ignore his earlier life, which was crowned by military success and considerable political and aesthetic accomplishments.

Yoshimoto was the third son of Imagawa Ujichika, and in 1536 secured his inheritance by a victory known as the Hanagura Incident. It involved the taking of Hanagura castle, which Yoshimoto did in a fine style that would not have disgraced any of his contemporaries. But the main enemy to the prosperity of the Imagawa house was to be Oda Nobuhide, father of the famous Oda Nobunaga. In 1542 Yoshimoto advanced into Owari province and met Nobuhide in battle at the first battle of Azukizaka. He was bloodily repulsed, and a few months later Oda Nobuhide followed up his victory by attacking the Imagawa fortress of Ueno. The castle held out, but only just. At this point the name of another famous father comes into the story, because shortly after the siege of Ueno a son was born to one of Imagawa Yoshimoto's allies, Tokugawa Hirotada; the boy would grow up to be the great Tokugawa Ieyasu. A few years later, Oda Nobuhide attacked Hirotada's castle of Okazaki. Hirotada appealed to Yoshimoto for help, which was granted on condition that the young Ieyasu be sent to the Imagawa castle of Sumpu as a hostage. This was agreed, but on the way the boy was kidnapped by Oda men. This put Hirotada into a dilemma in terms of conducting future campaigns against the Oda, but fortunately Imagawa Yoshimoto had no such qualms and went to war successfully. In 1549 he inflicted a considerable defeat upon Oda Nobuhide, who died shortly afterwards. Tokugawa Hirotada also died in that same year.

Yoshimoto was assisted in the above campaign by his talented uncle, the Zen monk Sessai Choro. One of Yoshimoto's greatest skills as a samurai commander was the ability to persuade others to do the fighting for him while he indulged in artistic pursuits, and Sessai Choro was the military anchor of his house. When Oda Nobuhide died, Sessai

太平記忠臣勇傳

稲川治部六天源義基

Imagawa Yoshimoto (1519–60), best known for his defeat at Okehazama, was a skilled samurai commander in his younger days.

Choro led the Imagawa army against the heir, Oda Nobuhiro, who was besieged inside Anjo castle. The attack was lifted when it was agreed that the Oda should return the hostage Tokugawa Ieyasu to the Imagawa. The future Shogun therefore made his way finally to Sumpu, set by the sea with the magnificent backdrop of Mount Fuji. Here, he was able to enjoy for the remainder of his boyhood the atmosphere of the 'little Kyoto' that Imagawa Yoshimoto had created in imitation of the court of his Ashikaga relatives in the capital, at which Yoshimoto held poetry and painting contests and performed the tea ceremony. As long as he had his uncle Sessai Choto to lead his armies and men like the Tokugawa to fight in them Yoshimoto prospered. But Sessai Choro died in 1555. Fortunately young samurai commanders like Tokugawa Ieyasu were growing in confidence. Ieyasu fought his first battle for

Imagawa Yoshimoto is killed at Okehazama in 1560. Yoshimoto was resting in a gorge and enjoying a head-viewing ceremony after his capture of a castle. Suddenly, under the cover of a fortuitous thunderstorm, Oda Nobunaga attacked and Yoshimoto was decapitated.

Imagawa Yoshimoto is seen here as a wooden statue at Okazaki castle. He is wearing court robes.

Yoshimoto in 1558 when he captured the castle of Terabe that had been handed over to Oda Nobunaga by its supposed keeper.

Over the next few years, Tokugawa Ieyasu was heavily involved in campaigns that were to provide the curtain raisers for Yoshimoto's ambitious plans for 1560. By that year there existed several *daimyo* like Hojo Ujiyasu and Takeda Shingen who possessed the military resources to begin the reunification of Japan. However, political or geographical factors meant that they had to concentrate instead on maintaining their own territories against their neighbours. Imagawa Yoshimoto was different. The location of his domains along the line of the Tokaido, the Eastern Sea Road, gave him a considerable advantage when it came to communications, so in 1560 he prepared to advance on Kyoto to make the latest Shogun bend to his will.

His first objective was the province of Owari, which was ruled by a minor *daimyo* called Oda Nobunaga, whose army the Imagawa outnumbered by 12 to one. At first all went well, and the Oda border fortresses tumbled before the Imagawa advance, but Yoshimoto grew complacent, and took a break to perform the traditional head-viewing ceremony in a small wooded ravine called Okehazama. Young Oda Nobunaga seized his chance, and attacked the Imagawa encampment under the cover of a fortuitous thunderstorm. Before Yoshimoto knew what was happening, his head had been lopped from his shoulders.

The brief battle of Okehazama put paid to all the Imagawa ambitions and raised the victorious Oda Nobunaga to the first rank of samurai commanders. The time of reunification had begun. From now on the whole face of samurai warfare was to change, and with it the role of the samurai commander.

Uesugi Kenshin (1530–78)

Uesugi Kenshin was not of the Uesugi family but was the son of their retainer, Nagao Tamekage, and bore the original name of Kagetora. When young Kagetora was 15 he was placed in joint command of Tochio castle. Here he was attacked by rebels against the Uesugi, but he soundly defeated them, earning the young man a reputation.

Kagetora entered the castle of Kasugayama as his father's heir at the age of 19. He was now head of the family and, although all-powerful and well respected in the immediate area of Kasugayama, he was still only a retainer of the Uesugi. But his masters had been in serious decline for many years, and it was inevitable that Kagetora should be making plans against the day when they finally relinquished power.

The Uesugi's main enemies had long been the Hojo, and when the Hojo defeated them once again in 1551, the Uesugi leader, Uesugi Norimasa, was forced to seek refuge with his followers. The obvious place to retreat to was Kasugayama, the castle of his leading vassal Nagao Kagetora and, when Norimasa came to him on bended knee, Kagetora agreed to protect his former overlord on his own, very strict terms. Uesugi Norimasa would have to adopt him as his heir, give him the name of Uesugi and the title of Echigo-no-kami (Lord of Echigo), and make him Kanto Kanrei (Shogun's deputy for the Kanto area). Norimasa had little choice but to agree to all these demands, so Nagao Kagetora was transformed into Uesugi Kagetora.

Kagetora shaved his head and took the name of Uesugi Kenshin in the following year of 1552. Under this name he fought many battles and was particularly renowned for his skills in fortress warfare. In 1552 the Shogun ordered him to make war upon the Hojo. As he was also under pressure from the Takeda at the time, he had to fight on two fronts. The most famous of his encounters with the latter were the five battles of Kawanakajima. His wars against the Hojo were more decisive, and by 1564 Kenshin controlled the provinces of Etchu and Kozuke. An alliance was made with the Hojo whereby Kenshin, who had no son, adopted Hojo Ujiyasu's son as his heir. Uesugi Kenshin also took on Oda Nobunaga, and inflicted a rare defeat on that renowned samurai commander in 1577. Oda Nobunaga was marching to the relief of Nanao castle in Noto province, then being besieged by Kenshin. Kenshin met Nobunaga's army at the Tedorigawa River. He cleverly arranged a decoy force to make Nobunaga think he had split his forces. This encouraged Nobunaga to make a fatal frontal assault across the river. The result was one of the classic night battles of Japan.

Kenshin finally died from an apopleptic fit in his lavatory in 1578, although his death was so fortuitous for Oda Nobunaga that assassination by a ninja was immediately suspected. The tale of how the ninja is supposed to have concealed

Uesugi Kenshin (1530–78), with his shaved head, enjoys a little relaxation in his castle of Kasugayama.

Uesugi Kenshin at the second
battle of Kawanakajima. Here he
is seen in prepared defensive
positions staring across the
Saigawa River at Shingen.

himself under Kenshin's lavatory and stabbed him from below is one of
the goriest stories of the samurai.

Takeda Shingen (1521–73)

Takeda Harunobu Shingen was born in 1521. 'Shingen' was the Buddhist
name that Harunobu took on becoming a monk in 1551. At the early
age of 15, in 1536, he received his baptism of fire as a samurai warrior
when his father, Nobutora, attacked a certain Hiraga Genshin at
Hiraga's fortress of Umi no kuchi. Takeda Nobutora attacked Umi no
kuchi with 8,000 troops, but was forced to retreat when there was a
heavy fall of snow. But in the small hours of the morning his enthusiastic
son struck camp and marched his men back to Umi no kuchi in secret.
They attacked and took the castle.

The incident showed how much more skilled Shingen was than his
father, who openly disliked him in spite of his victories, so on 7 July 1541
Takeda Harunobu deposed his father and took total control of Kai. It
is quite clear that the Takeda retainers largely approved of their young

Takeda Shingen (1521–73), looking characteristically fierce with an appearance likened to that of the god Fudo the Immovable.

lord taking over, and rallied round when the *daimyo* of neighbouring Shinano hurried to take advantage of the expected dissension in the Takeda camp. Their armies made a deep penetration into Kai within five days of the coup, but Harunobu was ready for them and used 5,000 farmers and tradesmen to make his army appear to be almost twice the size it actually was.

Takeda Shingen's personal life was conducted on a scale that was as flamboyant as his military activities. He had two principal wives and three mistresses, but they were outnumbered by possibly 30 others with whom he was intimate in a less formal sense. Several portraits of Shingen survive to show a consistently strong image. He was a solidly built, determined-looking man, portrayed in later life with elaborate

Takeda Shingen at the second battle of Kawanakajima. He is waiting for a move by Kenshin, and receives intelligence from one of his messengers.

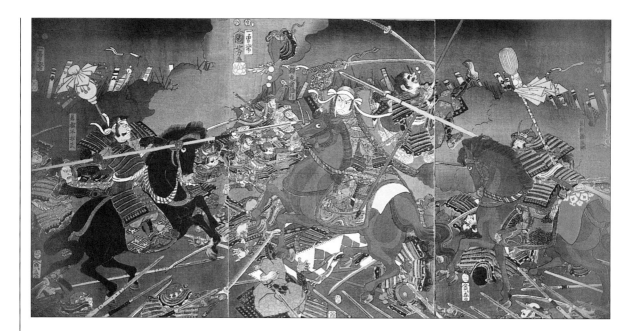

The single combat at the fourth battle of Kawanakajima. This anachronistic incident, shown here as dawn breaks, pitted the two greatest commanders of the age against one another.

side-whiskers. Takeda Shingen was also renowned for the successful way in which he governed his province. Kai was ruled from Kofu, then called Fuchu, but in spite of his military prowess his headquarters in Kofu was not a castle. Instead Shingen ruled from a *yashiki* (mansion) called Tsutsujigasaki. With a rectangular ground plan and defended only by a wet moat, its apparent weakness came to symbolize Shingen's confidence in his armies and his subjects to defend him, rather than placing his trust in stone walls.

Overall we see in Shingen an example of the classic Sengoku *daimyo*. He was skilled in war, a very good administrator, a skilled politician and a cultivated patron of the arts. He was also utterly determined and completely ruthless, slaughtering rival samurai and burning villages with contemptuous detachment. His campaigns at Kawanakajima are renowned, as was his skilful use of cavalry at Mikata ga Hara in 1572.

Of the five battles fought at Kawanakajima, none was contested more fiercely than the fourth battle in 1561. Shingen hoped to surprise Kenshin by crossing the Chikumagawa River in the middle of the night and setting up battle lines. The ranks would receive the fleeing Uesugi troops when a surprise dawn attack was launched on their rear. It was a brilliant plan, but Kenshin got wind of it and arranged his own surprise for Shingen. As dawn broke, the approaching Uesugi samurai were not fleeing in terror but bearing down upon the Takeda in a co-ordinated attack. Suddenly a mounted figure burst into the curtained enclosure that was Shingen's headquarters. It was Uesugi Kenshin himself, and for a few brief moments a single combat was fought between these two illustrious samurai commanders.

The encounter was a portent of the decline of these old-style samurai commanders. The battle of Kawanakajima was ultimately indecisive, and by the time the two rivals had settled their difference the political centre of gravity in Japan had shifted dramatically. There were new powers in the land, and new demands to be made upon a fresh generation of samurai commanders.

GLOSSARY

abumi	stirrups
agemaki	large ornamental bow on back of armour
bakufu	the government of the Shogun
bushidan	warrior bands
bushido	the code of chivalry
daimyo	feudal lords
do	body armour
eboshi	cap worn under the helmet
emishi	aborigines of the eastern lands
fukigayeshi	turnbacks on a helmet
fundoshi	loin cloth
gunkimono	war tales
hachimaki	head cloth
haidate	thigh guard
hara-kiri	ritual suicide
haramaki	armour opening at the back
hitatare	robe worn under armour
ikki uchi	single combat
kabuki	the popular theatrical form of the Edo period
kabuto	helmet
kami	the deities of Japan's religion of Shinto
kami-kaze	the 'divine wind' that sunk the Mongol fleet in 1281
kebiki odoshi	closed spaced lacing of armour
keiko	old style of armour
koku	unit of wealth of rice fields
kondei	powerful local landowner
kote	sleeves of armour
kumade	type of battle-axe with prongs
kusazuri	skirt pieces of armour
kuwagata	ornamental antlers on a helmet
kyuba no michi	horse and bow skills, the origin of *bushido*
kyusen no michi	the way of the bow and arrow
maku	semi-enclosed space provided by curtains on the battlefield
mikoshi	the sacred palanquin of the warrior monks in which the *kami* was believed to dwell
mon	heraldic badge or crest
monto	believers, followers of Jodo-Shinshu
motodori	pigtail
naginata	glaive
nodachi	long-bladed field sword
nodowa	throat protector
obi	under belt
o-yoroi	the most elaborate form of *yoroi* armour
oyumi	Japanese crossbow used in sieges up to the 12th century
samurai	the military elite of Japan
seppuku	*hara-kiri* or ritual suicide
shikken	the regency of the Hojo family
shugo	the Shogun's provincial deputy
sode	shoulder plates on armour

This woodblock print shows the classic image of the samurai commander. He is in full *yoroi* armour and carries a bow.

sohei	warrior monks
suneate	shin guards
tabi	socks with a separate compartment for a big toe
tachi	sword hung from the waist with the cutting edge downward
taisho	general
tanto	dagger
tengu	goblins of the forests
tsuba	sword guard
wako	Japanese pirate
waraji/zori	straw sandals
ya awase	arrow duel
yabusame	mounted archery competition
yamashiro	mountain castles
yoroi	classic style of armour
yoroi-hitatare	(see *hitatare*) armour robe
yugake	gloves

SELECT BIBLIOGRAPHY AND FURTHER READING

Aston, W. G., *Nihongi: Chronicles of Japan from the Earliest Times to AD 697,* Tuttle and Co., Vermont, 1972.

Conlan, Thomas, *State of War: The Violent Order of Fourteenth-Century Japan,* University of Michigan, Ann Arbor, 2003.

Friday, Karl, 'Valorous Butchers: The Art of War during the Golden Age of the Samurai', *Japan Forum* 5, 1993, pp.1–43.

Friday, Karl, *Samurai, Warfare and the State in Early Medieval Japan,* Routledge, London, 2004.

Ikegami, Eiko, *The Taming of the Samurai: Honorific Individualism and the Making of Modern Japan,* Harvard University Press, Cambridge, Mass., 1994.

Kitagawa, Hiroshi and Tsuchida, Bruce, *The Tale of Heike (Heike Monogatari),* University of Tokyo Press, Tokyo, 1975.

McCullough, Helen, *The Taiheiki: A Chronicle of Medieval Japan,* Columbia University Press, New York, 1959.

Morris, Ivan, *The Nobility of Failure: Tragic Heroes in the History of Japan,* Secker and Warburg, London, 1975.

Philippi, Donald L., *Kojiki,* University of Tokyo Press, Tokyo, 1969.

Rabonivitch, Judith (trans. and ed.), *Shomonki, the Story of Masakado's Rebellion,* Sophia University, Tokyo, 1986.

Seward, Jack, *Hara-kiri: Japanese Ritual Suicide,* Tuttle, Vermont, 1968.

Takegoshi, Y., *The Story of the Wako,* trans. by Hideo Watanabe, Kenkyusha, Tokyo, 1940.

Tanaka Taneo, 'Japan's Relations with Overseas Countries', in Hall and Toyoda (eds.), *Japan in the Muromachi Age,* University of California Press, Berkeley and Los Angeles, 1977, pp. 159–78.

Tsunoda R., de Bary W., Keene, D. (eds.), *Sources of Japanese Tradition Volume I* Columbia University Press, New York, 1958.

Varley, Paul, *Warriors of Japan as Portrayed in the War Tales,* University of Hawaii Press, Honolulu, 1994.

Wilson, William R., *Hogen Monogatari,* Sophia University Press, Tokyo, 1971.

Wilson, William R., 'The Way of the Bow and Arrow, the Japanese Warrior in *Konjaku Monogatari',* *Monumenta Nipponica* 28, 1973, pp.177–233.

Yoshinaka's victory at Kurikara in 1183 was helped along by his unusual stratagem of tying lighted torches to the horns of a herd of oxen and stampeding them into the midst of the Taira ranks.

THE PLATES

A: EARLY SAMURAI COMMANDERS

This plate shows the appearance of three great samurai commanders in the years leading up to the start of the Gempei Wars. All are wearing variations of the *yoroi* style of armour.

A1: Taira Masakado (c.903–40)

No contemporary illustrations of Masakado exist, so he is shown here in an elaborate suit of armour worn by another samurai commander in a contemporary illustration. It would have been completely appropriate for a man of Masakado's rank. His *kabuto* (helmet) has a typical low and heavy iron *hachi* (bowl). The rows of rivets can just be seen. It bears *kuwagata* of deer antlers. As Masakado has chosen to arm himself with a *naginata* (glaive) for a fight on foot rather than a bow he has retained two *kote* (armour sleeves), but has pulled the right sleeve of his *hitatare* (armour robe) out over his right arm. He is wearing the very heavy *o-tateage no suneate* (iron shin guards) and black bearskin boots. He has been closely engaged in the fighting, as shown by the fragment of his enemy's helmet that he has torn off!

A2: Minamoto Yoriyoshi (995–1082)

Yoriyoshi, the early hero of the Minamoto, is shown in more typical style of a samurai commander as he is mounted on a horse and carries a bow. He is wearing a magnificent red *o-yoroi* armour, and has discarded his right *kote* for ease in drawing a bow. His spare bowstring reel dangles beside his sword. On his back he wears a *horo*, the ornamental cloak reserved for important warriors. Sometimes it would be stretched over a bamboo frame, but Yoriyoshi has tied it around his waist.

A3: Minamoto Kiso Yoshinaka (1154–84)

Yoshinaka was a samurai from the central mountains of Japan and was regarded as vulgar compared to his contemporaries in Kyoto. The picture is based on a vivid painted scroll at the Gichuji in Otsu where he is buried. It is very lifelike, and shows him as a rough character. He has casually perched himself on a rock rather than a general's camp stool. He is nevertheless an imposing figure. His *yoroi*

has more and smaller *kusazuri* (skirt sections) than those of his companions. This was a variation found in the twelfth century, but the inclusion of simple *haidate* (thigh guards) is probably a mistake of the original painter. We have included it here for completeness.

B: SAMURAI COMMANDERS OF THE GEMPEI WARS

In this plate, two of the most famous rival generals of the Gempei Wars are shown in full battle action. The scene is the tragic battle of Dan no Ura in 1185, the sea battle in which the Taira were wiped out.

B1: Taira Tomomori (1152–85)

Taira Tomomori was unquestionably the greatest samurai commander his doomed family produced. He is seen here at the moment of his dramatic suicide by drowning after the Taira were defeated at the battle of Dan no Ura in 1185. Two variations of the story exist, one where he dons two suits of armour to weigh his body down, and the version shown here where he is shown holding on to a massive four-pronged iron anchor, about to leap into the sea. This is the traditional representation of the act depicted in kabuki drama and woodblock prints. Tomomori is shown in the classic pose of the defeated warrior. His dishevelled hair is streaming in the wind, unlike the neat appearance that samurai cherished. He is blood stained and arrows protrude from his armour. His torn *hitatare* (armour robe) shows the left sleeve of his *shitagi* (shirt).

B2: Minamoto Yoshitsune (1159–89)

Yoshitsune, the victor of Dan no Ura, is shown pursuing Tomomori, while around them the flags of the Taira float in the water. His shortness of stature is apparent. He is dressed in a magnificent *yoroi* armour with a helmet crest of a *komainu* (Chinese dog). His *tanto* (dagger) is firmly thrust into his belt.

C: THE LOYALIST COMMANDERS

The two greatest samurai commanders on the imperial loyalist side in the Nanbokucho Wars are shown here.

In this detail from the picture scroll of the Later Three Years' War we see Minamoto Yoshiie sitting in camp. At the close of each day's fighting, Yoshiie examined his men's exploits. The bravest warrior was assigned to the 'bravery seat' while the worst at fighting had to occupy a 'cowardice seat'.

C1: Kusunoki Masashige (1294–1336)

Few samurai have been more reproduced in illustrations than Masashige. This plate is based on a painted scroll in Wakayama castle. His helmet has a very striking front crest called a *mitsu-kuwagata*, with the sword of the god Fudo balancing the two ordinary *kuwagata* (antlers). His armour is the more modern *do-maru* style, and the absence of a leather cover to the breastplate is very noticeable. On his right *sode* (shoulder guard) he wears a small identifying flag bearing his famous 'chrysanthemum on the water' *mon* (badge).

C2: Nitta Yoshisada (1301–38)

Yoshisada, the victor of Kamakura in 1333, is dressed in a *yoroi* armour with a very fine *tsurubashiri* (leather cover to the breastplate – literally 'the path of the bowstring). He has not yet put his helmet on, so we can see his *eboshi* (cap) that would act as padding for the helmet. In the background we see the terrain around Chihaya, where hilltop defences placed new demands on samurai leadership. Their followers proudly display Kusunoki Masashige's banner.

D: ASHIKAGA TAKAUJI (1305–58)

Ashikaga Takauji was the first Ashikaga Shogun. This plate is based on a contemporary painting of a mounted samurai general that has long been traditionally regarded as representing Takauji. The picture actually bears the cipher of the second Shogun Ashikaga Yoshiakira (1330–68), but this may simply indicate that Yoshiakira commissioned the painting of his illustrious father.

Whoever is represented, and Ashikaga Takauji must be the most likely subject, it is a perfect illustration of a leading samurai commander of the time. The details of the armour and equipment are exactly right for the mid-fourteenth century. Takauji is shown bareheaded and carrying a very striking *seiro-dachi*, a long sword half way between the standard *tachi* and the extra long *nodachi*. It has a large openwork *tsuba* (sword guard). He is wearing a *yoroi* armour laced with white silk very similar to those worn during the Gempei Wars, but he is wearing two *kote* instead of one. He is still a mounted archer, however, in addition to being a swordsman, because he has an *ebira* (quiver) and a spare bowstring reel hangs from his belt. His *yugake* (archery gloves) are of patterned brown leather. His other sword is inside a scabbard ornamented with tiger skin. The details of his leg protection are most interesting. He wears the heavy iron *suneate* (shin guards) of an earlier time, but his *hakama* (breeches) are armoured with small metal plates.

The battle of Dan no Ura as shown on a painted screen in the Akamagu shrine in Shimonoseki, the site of the battle.

In attendance on Takauji are his helmet bearer and his flag bearer. Both wear *haramaki* (armour opening at the back) and the rigid form of the *eboshi*. The flag bearer holds Takauji's white banner bearing the paulownia *mon* of the Ashikaga family.

E: SAMURAI COMMANDERS OF THE ONIN WAR

The two rivals of the Onin War are shown here against a background of the devastation their conflict caused in Kyoto, which has been turned into a wasteland. Fierce *ashigaru* (footsoldiers) charge down the hill.

E1: Yamana Sozen Mochitoyo (1404–73)

Yamana Sozen is wearing armour that shows the transition to the Age of Warring States. His body defence is a splendid *haramaki* armour with a large *nodowa* (throat ring), but he is not wearing a helmet. Instead his shaven head shows his status as a monk, and his red face provides the characteristic by which he was best known. Instead of a bow he carries a sword, and is wearing two *kote* (sleeves) and heavy *haidate* (thigh guards). His *suneate* (shin guards) are still the old-fashioned heavy iron type.

E2: Hosokawa Katsumoto (1430–73)

Katsumoto is shown in action. He is wearing a *do-maru* armour to which he has added a rather old-fashioned looking helmet. He is loosing his bow, and the arrows in his *ebira* (quiver), tied round his waist, may be seen behind him. His two *kote* (sleeves) are simple cloth bags with chain mail and small plates added, so they are flexible enough to allow him to draw his bow.

F: SAMURAI COMMANDERS OF THE EARLY SENGOKU PERIOD

Here is a contrast in fortunes. We have two samurai commanders who experienced very different fates.

F1: Hojo Soun (1432–1519)

Soun was the first of five generations of the Hojo who ruled from Odawara castle. Like Yamana Sozen he was a monk, but over his shaved head he wears one form of a monk's cowl instead of a helmet. This picture is based on a contemporary painted scroll of Soun that is kept in Odawara castle. His armour is a *yoroi* – an old-fashioned choice that makes him appear like a commander from the Gempei Wars. He also retains the heavy *suneate* and bearskin boots. Behind him flies the proud banner of the Hojo.

F2: Togashi Masachika (died 1488)

No painting of the unfortunate Togashi Masachika has survived, so we have chosen to show him here wearing a contemporary *do-maru* armour laced in close-spaced *kebiki-odoshi* style. He carries an impressive lacquered quiver. His helmet has a gold helmet badge representing a *gohei*, the sacred 'wand' of Shinto. He wears a face mask, an important innovation of the times. In place of the bearskin boots he has simple straw sandals.

All this was not enough to save him from his fate at the hands of the Ikko-ikki of Kaga, who are shown in the background. They are a peasant army, and even their banner, with its evocation of Amida Buddha, is made from a straw curtain.

G: SHIMAZU TAKAHISA (1514–71)

Under Shimazu Takahisa the Shimazu family of Satsuma entered the wider world of Japanese and international politics. Satsuma was the gateway for guns and Christianity, and became Japan's first province to have contacts with Europe. Takahisa was also a skilled general, and it is his role as a samurai commander that is depicted here. He is leading the attack on the fortress of Iwatsurugi in 1554. This was a *yamashiro* (mountain castle) approachable only by steep and narrow paths, up which the Shimazu samurai doggedly fought their way.

The reproduction of Takahisa is based on two very reliable sources. The first is an equestrian portrait owned by Kagoshima City Art Museum. This was painted during the

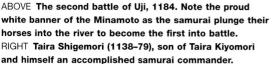

ABOVE **The second battle of Uji, 1184. Note the proud white banner of the Minamoto as the samurai plunge their horses into the river to become the first into battle.**
RIGHT **Taira Shigemori (1138–79), son of Taira Kiyomori and himself an accomplished samurai commander.**

OPPOSITE **The great honour of being the first into battle often caused competition among samurai. At the second battle of Uji in 1184 two samurai raced their horses across the river.**

sixteenth century by an artist who had access to Takahisa's actual armour, which still exists and is kept by the Reimeikan in Kagoshima. It is an *iro iro odoshi do-maru* (multi-coloured lacing *do-maru* style armour). The *do-maru* fastened under the right armpit. The three colours used for the bands of the lacing are purple, crimson and white. The shoulder guards, laced in the same way, are the large *o-sode* type. Two small metal plates, heavily ornamented, protect the suspensory cords of the armour over the shoulders. His *kabuto* (helmet) is of *suji-bachi* (ridged bowl) construction and is fitted with a *maedate* (helmet crest) in the form of the sword of Fudo. This perfectly balances the *kuwagata* (antlers). The *shikoro* is shallow, typical of the age where fighting with edged weapons was favoured over bows. Takahisa's weapon of choice is a *naginata* (glaive). He wears heavy iron *suneate* (shin guards), but has simple straw sandals on his feet.

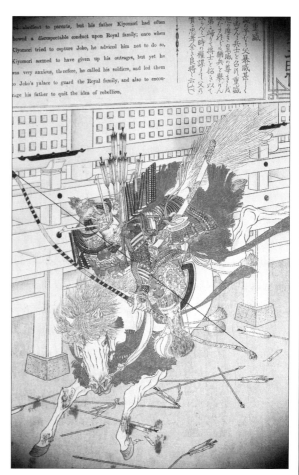

His follower is wearing a leather covered armour and carrying a fierce *nodachi* sword. In the background looms the wooded hill on which Iwatsurugi castle is built, with Shimazu flags to the fore.

H: THE FOURTH BATTLE OF KAWANAKAJIMA

This plate reproduces the famous anachronistic single combat between Uesugi Kenshin and Takeda Shingen at the fourth battle of Kawanakajima in 1561. It is taken from one of many woodblock prints that deal with the subject. In the background are two of the most important flags of the Takeda.

H1: Takeda Shingen (1521–73)

Shingen is shown being surprised by Kenshin's attack and rising from his tiger-skin covered camp stool. He is trying to defend himself using his war fan, which has the design of star constellations on it. He is wearing a helmet with a large horse hair plume and a *maedate* (crest) of two *kuwagata* and a grinning *oni* (devil) face. He wears a long-sleeved red *jinbaori* (surcoat).

H2: Uesugi Kenshin (1530–78)

Wielding his sword, Kenshin crashes into the Takeda camp. He is wearing a decorative *kataginu* (a sleeveless coat lighter than a *jinbaori*). Kenshin was also a Buddhist monk, so he is wearing a variation on the monk's cowl that tied round the face.

INDEX